FROM THE COCKPIT

FROM THE COCKPIT
Coming *of* Age in the Korean War

BY

TEX ATKINSON

JOHN M. HARDY PUBLISHING

ALPINE & HOUSTON

2 0 0 4

First Printing: July 2004

1 3 5 7 9 10 8 6 4 2

ISBN 0-9717667-4-6

Printed and Bound in the United States of America

Cover Design - Leisha Israel, Blue Sky Media
Austin, Texas

All photography from the collections of Tex Atkinson or
the US Navy

Tunnel Bombing painting by Morgan Wilbur

Hill County Courthouse drawing by Blair Arnold

Portions of "Tunnel Busting in Korea" taken from Tex
Atkinson's previously published article in *Naval Aviation News*

Excerpt from *All Over But The Shoutin'* by Rick Bragg, copyright
© 1997 by Rick Bragg. Used by permission of Pantheon Books, a
division of Random House, Inc.

John M. Hardy Publishing Company
Houston, Texas

www.johnmhardy.com

To that silent group who fought, suffered, and died so that millions in South Korea might live a lifetime of freedom, this book is most respectfully dedicated.

Preface

If the Korean War had played on Broadway, it would have been one of the great flops of all time. The opening date of June 25, 1950, was remarkably bad timing — only five years after the end of World War II. The millions who fought and survived that pandemonium were desperately trying to build a new life and forget the chaos from which millions had not survived. Korea? Whoever heard of the place?

So when President Harry Truman ordered American troops to Korea via the United Nations, the majority of our nation read the headlines, muttered something like "Old Harry! He's got his dander up again," and went back to the business at hand. Some were completing their education, using their GI-Bill benefits. Others were starting a new family. Companies that had stashed profits during the war were expanding. Other new companies were starting. Fresh technology was bursting at the seams, eager to be developed: plastics, rayon, Tucker and Kaiser-Frazer automobiles, jet airplanes, something called TV, and new sophisticated calculators that would grow up to be computers. And hanging like a dark cloud over all was the beginning of a New Age called "Atomic."

Few, if any, were interested in a new war. But despite the bad timing the show opened. It played for three years, killed over 40,000 of our fighting men, and closed quietly where it started — along a man-made line called the 38th parallel.

The war was fought by United Nations forces, by North and South Koreans, and by Chinese and Russians. The preponderance of the United Nations' forces was US military men. Many were veterans from World War II who had remained in the service. But most were young draftees, and still others were reservists recalled from civilian life.

In name, our forces were about the same as we have today. The Army sent several divisions. The Navy was there with carriers and battleships, with destroyers and tankers and hospital ships. The same Marines who made beach landings in the Pacific just a few years before would make landings in Korea. The flying branch of the Army — called the Army Air Force by the end of World War II — now dropped the Army label and became the US Air Force.

All would see action and all would suffer casualties, but not many would write about their experiences. Libraries today have few books on the subject of the Korean War. Public knowledge of the war has come in the main from the entertainment media — the TV series *M*A*S*H*, and a James Michener book and movie titled *The Bridges at Toko Ri*. I do not recall an episode of *M*A*S*H* that mentioned Navy carrier pilots.

My entry into the war was on December 5, 1950, when I made my first combat flight. The mission was close air support near the Chosin Reservoir in Korea. An estimated 100,000 Chinese surrounded fewer than 20,000 US Marine and Army troops in the mountains of northeast Korea. Seventy miles down a narrow mountain road was the only way out. Night and day the high ground atop steep cliffs had to be cleared of tough, hard-fighting Chinese soldiers. In the areas of most intense combat, five-to-one odds and higher favored the bad guys. Fifty-mile-an-hour winds, snow storms, temperatures of minus 30 at night, little if any sleep, bugles and whistles in the dark, frozen bodies stacked and used as sand bags — usually theirs, sometimes ours — all were a constant reminder of sudden or slow death. Either could be waiting at the next bend in the road.

Our squadron and many others flew every hour of every day that weather would permit, and sometimes when it did not. Waiting at the end of the trail was the harbor of Hungnam. Air controllers in battle-scarred buildings fired smoke flares to target our bombs only one city block from tired men fighting to make that last mile to waiting ships. Evacuation was completed on Christmas Eve.

Good men died trying to escape the Chosin. A lot of them. Their deaths did settle one matter: no doubt remained that China had entered the United Nations Peace Action.

On June 23, 1952, I flew "section" (the third aircraft in a division of four) with Art Downing, Carrier Air Group Commander (CAG) of Air Group Two. CAG led three air groups, each containing three divisions of AD dive-bombers plus jet cover, from three carriers. This was the largest assemblage of carrier aircraft for combat since World War II. Our target was the Suhio hydroelectric plant, only 35 miles from a huge concentration of Soviet MiG-15 fighters based at Antung airfield. Suhio was the largest of the North Korean hydroelectric plants.

Many historians now agree that protection of these vital sources of power was one of China's primary concerns in Korea. Their destruction in June of 1952 brought darkness to large parts of Manchuria and North Korea. The armistice was signed in 1953.

I have never talked with a single person actively involved in the war who did not believe our fight was necessary to stop Communist domination of additional millions in Asia, the Far East, and the Pacific Basin. Had this happened, our world today would be different. A comparison of contemporary North and South Korea reveals in graphic detail what that difference would have been.

Those with whom I flew were a unique group of people. Most of us wanted to be where we were. Not necessarily fighting a war. We just wanted to fly. We were not bitter because of the lack of attention back home. The youngest of us were in high school during World War II, enjoying the benefits of being outnumbered by good-looking girls. We were well aware that most of our country, at the time of Korea, was thinking only of settling down. "A little plastic palace in Dallas" are words from a popular song of the era.

The years from World War II until the beginning of the

1960s were, for most of us, sweet and special years. A lot happened other than a conflict in Korea. Most of what happened was good.

The world, especially this country, seemed to be pausing, taking long deep breaths, sipping cool clear water, reflecting on a time — the forties — when mankind nearly lost all that we enjoy today. Our country, and indeed much of mankind, deserved a break, and while many of those who had run the race rested, others were preparing for that which was to come. It is a time worth recording.

Effective communication can be difficult at times, and during this apprenticeship as a first-time book author I ran into "writer's block." My youngest son, Greg, who is the real writer in the family, heard of my problem and sent me a great book written by Pulitzer winner Rick Bragg titled, *All Over But the Shoutin'*.

I read the book in a single sitting, could not put it down, and during the night my wife rolled and tossed and said more than once, "That must be some book you are reading." And it was.

I had hardly begun the book when I read how Rick was in New Orleans doing a feature story for the New York Times and was interviewing an elderly black lady in the ghettos who had just lost her grandson in a senseless shooting. He described how the little boy's "Dr. Seuss" books just dropped to the ground and the grandson died looking up at his grandmother with a shocked expression, unable to speak a word.

When the interview was over, the grandmother thanked Mr. Bragg for taking the time to write about her grandson.

Rick said that his normal reply to such a response from someone consumed with grief is simply to say "Thank you" and leave. But in this instance he replied, "Why in the world do you want to thank me? All I have done is to scribble a few notes. Your grandson is gone forever and you are the one who will live with his loss for the rest of your life."

The grandmother replied by showing him a few carefully folded clippings from New Orleans newspapers. The little pieces of paper, coldly and briefly, reported the story of her grandson's tragic death.

Then the grandmother said to Rick Bragg, "You sees, sir, if it ain't writ down, peoples forgets."

Screams stopped the ground controller in mid-sentence. "MAYDAY! MAYDAY! I'M ON FIRE! I'M ON FIRE!"

All radio chatter stopped. Flying Dave's wing in the AD, I could see that he was searching for the caller. Then we saw him. The Corsair was close, a mile or so ahead, low to the ground in a shallow dive. Orange-red flames reached from the rear of the engine back past the cockpit and blue gulled wings. Heavy black smoke trailed behind, drifting down toward dirty snow-covered ground.

Again the screams. Now louder, more desperate. "I'M

ON FIRE! I'M ON FIRE!" Sheer terror in a young voice without time to prepare for sudden death.

Then, abrupt silence as the Corsair disintegrated into a long trail of flame stretching across a rough, battle-scared field. Unmoving, a hunk of rolled blackened metal lay where the flames stopped.

Total quiet held for a brief moment. Then the gentle chatter of other flights continued. Our controller's voice picked up without change. "Tiger One, I am firing red for effect. Commence your run when ready."

Dave turned my way. I could see him clearly. We held eye contact for a second, then Dave wiped his forehead with his forefinger, shook his head slightly, passed the lead with a casual salute, and began his run.

Thus did we spend most of Sunday, Christmas Eve day, 1950. The evacuation of surviving US Marines and Army from Hungnam harbor was completed by dark. The battle of the Chosin Reservoir was ended. Ensign Hugo Scarsheim, his last transmission, and the Chosin, remain only as a memory in the minds of a few.

The next day atop an old gray metal table in front of our squadron's ready-room there was a small Christmas tree. Someone's mother had mailed the tree in a cake box. Flakes of white powder from the cake stuck to the little green leaves. All in all, quite nice. It added something to the day.

Chapter 1

On a clear night the glow of lights atop the rise of ground that is Hillsboro, Texas, can be seen for many miles. If you are driving, see the lights, and are the type who enjoys a quiet retreat, you will want to exit the new Interstate. Fast lanes of impersonal rush take you close to important places, but not to them.

As you get closer, you will be able to see the outline of the old courthouse that sits on the highest of the low rolling hills. That is when you should lower your windows, forget for the moment that air-conditioning was ever invented, and welcome the freshness of evening air. If it happens that you have lucked onto a really special night in late spring or early summer, then the fragrance of cotton blossoms will blend with the scents of cattle and grain. The perfume from wild flowers that replaced spring blankets of bluebonnets and Indian paintbrush will wash the night air. All will blend into a mellow relaxation that produces a fleeting sensation of what man's imagined heaven might be. You will have discovered one of those moments you will want to hold inside for as long as you can.

If you were born here, if you did the important part of your growing up here, if you first fell in love here, then you might have, on some special moonlit night, pulled an old Model-A Ford into a deserted grass-covered open space. Then you would have gotten out to stand in perfect stillness alongside an abandoned farm road so that you could be a part of the quietness. And you might have let your mind ramble freely, taking deep breaths and thinking about all the things you wanted to do with your life. And if you did these things, then Hillsboro could become a part of you. And if you were young and if you were sensitive, you could file that part away — the part that was Hillsboro — so that it would be there for you.

Hillsboro would be there when close friends became only memories of aircraft crashes at sea, or burning hunks of metal half buried in a Korean rice paddy, or a large cloud of black smoke and orange flame where a second ago there had been an aircraft just like yours. Hillsboro would be there when you were still flying, and your engine was purring with power and the controls felt solid, and you looked again when the smoke cleared and your buddy was gone. Hillsboro would forever be a place you could go to in your mind when you wondered why things happened the way they did.

All of these things I did, and Hillsboro was there through all the many years ahead — when my first love said "No," and when the "No" haunted me for too many years, until a happy marriage made it go away.

So long as I could hold onto my memories of the sweet cotton-blossomed night air that was Hillsboro, and so long as I compelled myself to become quiet and take deep breaths, then Hillsboro would be there. Again, I could park the old Model-A alongside a quiet country road, look across and see Janice, and behind in the rumble-seat Gus and Maxine, all grinning and laughing like Hillsboro had just beaten Waco thirty to six. The score was the opposite but we smiled anyway, because Hillsboro had beaten Waco only once in the past 30 years and that was in 1936 when E.L. Keeton was playing. Now, in 1945, everybody knew that Waco High would be the State Football Champion that year because the city of Waco was getting so big, still with only one High School, and in a year or two Hillsboro would not have to play Waco ever again. At least not in a game of football. So, what the hell.

When I was born in 1928, pilots flying old mail-planes over Hillsboro could look north and make out two distinct glows of light. The glow to the west was Ft. Worth and the glow to the east was Dallas. In between lay 30 miles of blackness. By the time I made my first flight at night over Hillsboro, the two glows of light had begun to join. Lights from Grand Prairie, where the Navy trained pilots in World War II, and lights from other new towns, added a fresh radiance to the miles of darkness. The last time I made a night flight over Hillsboro I looked north and studied the solid glow of brightness. I could not help but remember some of all the many things that had happened while those lights were multiplying.

I was born only a few blocks from the booming sound of the old clock in the tower of the Hill County courthouse, which still covers nearly all of a large city block in the center of downtown Hillsboro. Gus Hilton, who would become my best friend in high school, and who would join the Navy's flight program with me, at least for the college part, was born a few months after me. He, too, came into a world made mellower by the resounding knell of the old courthouse clock.

Hillsboro, Texas, in the 1930s and '40s was a great place in which to grow up. Gus was lucky; he got to spend all of his growing-up years there. My folks moved a lot. From the time I was born, I was in and out of Hillsboro several times for short stays, but it was not until I was in my last two years of high school that I was able to live there full time. 1944 and 1945 were good years to be a kid. Gus and I and many other young men were still in school, playing football and enjoying the benefits of being outnumbered by good-looking girls, while thousands upon thousands of guys just a few years older were overseas, fighting one of the most deadly wars in modern history.

The '30s were tough Depression years for the entire country and Hillsboro was not excluded. Franklin Roosevelt was elected President by the Depression-poor because his powerful and trusting voice, wonderfully clear, came pouring forth from the speakers of millions of small radios with a frank and simple message: he would stop the suffering and heal the pain. The poor believed, and his New Deal came to power in 1932. I was four years old then and do not recall a lot of detail. But I can remember when I was five or six that Roosevelt's framed, brown-tinted picture hung over the stand-up Victrola that stood in one corner of what served as our living room in a little cotton-mill house in Itasca, a small town 10 miles north of Hillsboro.

There was an NRA sign in our window and my memory paints it red, white, and blue. I still have the old faded Roosevelt picture, and the stand-up Victrola, but have no idea as to what happened to the sign that announced the birth of our country's National Recovery Act. I do still have a copy of an old cartoon printed in a New York Republican paper. It shows two little kids in front of a Long Island mansion. The little boy has written ROOSEVELT in big letters on the sidewalk and his sister is screaming so their parents can hear, "Mama! Papa! Johnny just wrote a nasty word!"

My mother and father were divorced when I was still a baby, and my mother and I moved in with Grandmother Atkinson. Strange that my father's family should adopt my mother and me, but that is the way it happened. My mother and grandmother worked in the cotton mill in Itasca for 50 cents a day when there was work, and somehow we survived.

Cotton-mill towns in mid-century had a character all their own. Like other factory towns all across our nation, they took in raw material at one end (in Itasca it was bales of cotton) and at the other end delivered the finished product, rolls of cloth ready for shipment.

In between the bales of raw cotton and the rolls of finished cloth were rows and rows of looms and workers who did the weaving. Other workers, always moving, always with their little bag of tools, kept the looms in working order. The air inside the mill was a fine mist of cotton fiber. If the mill made blue denim cloth, as they did in a god-forsaken mill in Waco, everything — workers, looms, and factory — was covered with blue lint. In both Itasca and Hillsboro the cloth was always white. The lint was always white. Thus in Itasca and Hillsboro, folks were of the very firm opinion that Hill County was a nicer place to work.

Some of my earliest memories are singing at the top of my voice in the mill's little protestant church on Sunday nights. Just about everybody that worked at the mill was always there. Later, when I was of early school age, I can remember walking down the main street of the mill-block in the warmth of a summer evening listening to Amos and Andy, Fibber Magee and Molly, Jack Benny, or any of the other great radio shows of the time. Every house would have its front door and windows open, and the sound of the same program could be heard as you moved down the street. You could go from one end of the street to the other and never miss a word!

It was a dull duck hunter's day in Corpus Christi. The year was 1954. A low-hanging stratus restricted all flying. Even airline-types were grounded, drinking coffee and calling for weather.

At NAAS Cabaniss a gung-ho Marine F6F instructor used the dead time to drill his students in aborted take-offs. Others, including Navy pilots in the adjoining hanger, lounged around acey-deucey boards. Tower chatter on the duty officer's radio provided background. When the

Marine flight was in position for practice, some intellectual in our group changed the radio channel so that we could hear conversation between the Marine instructor and his students. As I say, it was a dull day.

None of the trainees we were listening to that day had actually flown the aircraft in which they practiced. The F6F Hellcat was a high-powered, single-seat fighter. There was no way to give dual instruction in the Hellcat, as there had been in the two-seat SNJ trainer they had flown in Pensacola.

To prepare, the students had been given a lot of taxi time in the F6 and were now learning to handle the aircraft with full power. To master this new skill they were directed to add power smoothly until the throttle was full forward; they could then feel the powerful torque of the engine.

They were told what to expect and how to control direction when the fighter tried to swerve off the runway. They were instructed to cut power well before the fighter became airborne.

Everything was routine during the first aborted take-offs by the seven fledglings. They cut their power way too soon.

Then Marine Cadet H.D. "Danny" Parker came around for his second attempt. The instructor assumed his role as a coach.

"All right you guys, I want to see some improvement. Parker, show these fainthearteds how it's done. Hold full power until you hear me say CUT! Got it?"

Danny Parker, a soon-to-be Marine fighter pilot, was not about to miss his cue. "Yes Sir!" he replied, in a voice that told his instructor in no uncertain terms that here was a Marine who could follow orders.

Then Danny added full power. He let the Hellcat gain enough speed to get the tail off the ground.

"Cut Power," called the instructor.

The F-6 gained more speed.

"CUT POWER!"

The F-6 began to rotate.

"CUT POWER!! CUT POWER!!!" screamed the instructor.

All Danny Parker heard was, "POWER! POWER! POWER!"

The F-6 disappeared into gray soup. Acey-deucey boards were shoved aside.

I learned the basic facts by listening to tower radio and emergency channel while it was happening. The details I got that night from Danny Parker over drinks. Danny had dated my wife's sister for a while in primary flight training in Pensacola. Since coming to Cabaniss, he sometimes came over for home cooking.

When Danny's F6F left the ground, he knew he was in serious trouble. He was a typical Pensacola SNJ graduate of his day — he had about 200 hours of flying time and enough instrument time to "Taxi Cavu." (That's irreverent pilot lingo meaning that such a qualification authorized a young pilot to taxi when the weather was perfect, ceiling and visibility unlimited, but he was not well qualified to actually takeoff and fly an aircraft in instrument weather.)

When Danny realized he was airborne and comprehended that on his first flight in the F6F he must rely solely on instruments, a sudden burst of adrenaline shot through his system. He pushed his mike to say something but discovered that his lips were stuck solidly together. He then concentrated only on keeping his wings level and climbing. "No touch nothing," was his only thought.

When he passed 1000 feet he took a chance; he reduced power, then focused his mind on producing enough saliva to spit.

Shortly after Danny's Hellcat disappeared into the low clouds, his instructor gave control of his other students to another pilot, received clearance from the tower, and was in the air. He was on instruments and climbing to get on top of the clouds. He communicated with the tower and traffic control on "guard channel," a frequency reserved for serious emergencies.

Danny had by now managed to relax enough that he could produce a little salvia in his mouth. He thought he might be able to separate his stuck lips and talk. To test, he pushed the mike button and spit into the mike.

The tower called the instructor, "That's it. We think he went in."

Then an excited voice: "This is Parker. I didn't crash. I'm still in the air." The exhilaration in Danny Parker's voice left no doubt that he was still very much alive.

That fact was all that was needed. Experienced Navy and Marine aviation knowledge took charge; unscheduled confusion was quickly changed into routine and proven know-how.

Danny's instructor established communications with him and together they "reviewed the situation." After a short time, Danny's voice was as calm and confident as his instructor's. They were then able to climb into beautiful weather above the clouds. Once there, they made visual contact with each other and rendezvoused.

With plenty of gas in both aircraft, and with his newly rescued student snugly on his wing, the instructor and Danny waited for the weather to clear enough for a safe landing. They logged F-6 time.

Later, the instructor brought Danny in for a "two-squeak" landing. A few of us instructors formed a small welcome-back committee for the two returning heroes. Another alert and thoughtful member of our group had used the waiting time to prepare a special award for Danny Parker. So that you understand the significance of the award, I add a little background.

During the 1950s the "Green Card" was the highest instrument rating that could be achieved by a Navy or Marine pilot. The Air Force had a similar qualification. Once a pilot achieved this status they could sign their own clearance to fly in any weather. In pilot lingo the "Green Card" was interpreted to mean: "If you think you can hack it, Go!" Our thinking communicator presented his carefully prepared plaque to Danny:

AWARDED TO "HOT DAMN PARKER"
HONORARY GREEN CARD INSTRUMENT RATING

We then gave a little round of applause while Danny and his instructor flashed wide grins. Intellectuals will always find something to do. Even on a dull day. However, in looking back, I note that we were not quite as sharp as I like to remember. We forgot to cut off Danny Parker's tie. It was, after all, the occasion of his first solo in the F6F.

Chapter 2

Ialso had another family. My father's oldest sister, my Aunt Milly, was married to my Uncle John Laney. They had two sons — Billy, three years older than I, and Wiley, younger. I became the middle brother. South of Hillsboro, not far from Waco, my Uncle John ran a cotton gin seven miles east of Mart, Texas. The little community was called Victoria. The tiny settlement at the crossing of two dirt farm roads could be traveled only by foot or horseback during many cold rainy weeks in winter. It should not be confused with the better known Victoria, Texas, a small city northeast of Corpus Christi.

My Aunt Millie and Uncle John's Victoria, our Victoria, consisted only of the huge cotton gin, a very old one-story rambling farm house, a country grocery store next to the gin, and a one-room school house a quarter of a mile down the road that led to Mart. The many rooms and two kitchens in the old farmhouse, which seemed to have grown out of the ground sometime during the previous hundred years, filled one side of the wide clearing that allowed wagonloads of cotton to be pulled under the shed of the cotton gin. The extra space in the old house allowed my aunt to provide room and board for the workers when needed, and for the single "young-maid" schoolteacher who taught first through sixth grade in the one-room schoolhouse. The grocery store was at the crossroads on the other side of the gin. Inside there were always different flavors of Nehi soda buried in ice, and outside there was a hand-operated gasoline pump for the occasional Model-T or Model-A, Chevrolet, or John Deere farm tractor that might stop by for a few gallons.

It is all plowed under now. Cotton covers the ground for as far as you can see, and in the fall huge machines replace the bent-over pickers pulling their long white sacks and us kids earning school-clothes money for the first few weeks after school started, and then having to catch up when the picking season ended. The last time I drove my Uncle John out to the site that was once our Victoria, not long before he died, we could find only parts of the stone foundation where the weather-beaten gin house had once stood. Gone forever was the huge living room with the pot-bellied stove sitting in the center, the one that got red-hot on cold winter nights. The glow from the old stove and light from two or three kerosene lamps provided the little light we needed while we listened to an aged battery-powered Sears and Roebuck radio, whose battery always ran low just at the best part of Gang Busters. Then we would press our ears right up against the speaker to hear the ending.

My Uncle John was also the automobile mechanic for the area. When ginning season was over and the long nights of winter set in, John would oftentimes bring his huge tool box into the living room, spread newspapers on the hardwood floor and carefully set a large greasy engine on them so that he could work away grinding valves, putting in new rings, or rebuilding a carburetor while us kids listened to the radio.

Sometimes the young schoolteacher, who boarded with us in the winter, would join us. She was a very pretty girl in her early twenties. Her name was Miss Shaw, and she was engaged to an older man who owned the picture show in Mart. He would come on weekends to take her on dates. Knowing that we kids seldom got a chance to see a real movie, she would sometimes assign a historical movie that tied in with our studies as our homework. Then, using the skills of womanhood with her fiancé, she would arrange nickel passes for us. I can still remember old classics from the '30s like *Elizabeth and Essex*, *Mutiny on the Bounty*, and Errol Flynn's *Sea Hawk* — exciting movies that also taught a bit of history. All thanks to Miss Shaw.

There were usually a total of about 20 students in the room. At various times I sat in most of her six rows. She would give an assignment to one row, then move on to the next. It was always interesting to listen to what was going on in the other grades, particularly those a few rows ahead. On occasion, during those long winter evenings, Miss Shaw would take time to answer Billy's and my questions when we were trying to learn ahead. During these times I would sit as close to her as I could and soak in the sweet scent of her perfume. Billy would do the same, and afterwards when Wiley (who was too little to hear such talk) was not around, Billy and I would discuss and speculate as to what it must be like to be old enough to date a pretty girl on weekends.

Also gone are the huge cold rooms where we three kids jumped onto a high four-poster bed and climbed between ice-cold sheets beneath thick cotton quilts after being sent to bed from the cozy comfort of the big room. Finally, after wiggling ourselves deep into the folds of a feather mattress, the chill would slowly leave, and then we could hear the loud whistling of a Texas "norther" outside. The wind squealed and groaned, searching every crack in the old house, and now and then the sounds would change into little probing creaks and murmurs as the cold, too, searched for a way to join the comfort beneath our blankets.

The next morning we would wake slowly to the smell of Aunt Milly's hot biscuits and white gravy and fried salt-bacon, all cooking away, the smell drifting through the long hall that led down the center of the house to the kitchen. All of these things, too, are plowed under now, but layers of black dirt cannot bury memories.

The cotton gin was a wonderful play-yard for my two brother-cousins and me and for half a dozen neighbor kids from nearby farms. After the ginning season was over, the bales of cotton were stacked atop a platform in back waiting to be hauled by truck and wagon to cotton mills. Pieces of hard, tough, sharp-pointed hulls that were left by the pickers had been separated from the cotton and sucked by a huge pipe that dropped them into a monstrous mound to one side of the gin. There they sat, season after season, rotting and degenerating into a stinking pile of damp compost, where spiders and rats and an occasional snake would gather — all sorts of moving creatures to attract the interest of small boys. The great pile of strange critters and stranger smells was a constant challenge to climb, or to try riding a bicycle to the top, or riding a calf, or any other machine or animal that we could catch.

Soft cottonseed also had been separated from the cotton, and it was stored in a round silo about 30 feet high, which was divided into pie-shaped storage areas so that one farmer's seed was kept apart from another. Inside, the silo was pitch-blackness. Jumping into a totally dark pie-shaped storage bin — not knowing how far down you would fall before hitting softness — was a temptation that no kid could pass by. Finally, the inevitable happened. Our friend, Lonnie, the smallest seven-year-old in school, jumped into an empty bin and busted his arm and one leg real bad. That was the end of our jump-school days.

My best memories of the many times I lived with my Aunt Milly and my Uncle John, sometimes for a whole school year, are the model airplanes that my cousin Billy and I would build. Wiley was small, and although he joined in as much as older brothers would allow, he was still very young and Big Little Books about Dick Tracy and Tailspin Tommy, and radio programs such as *Little Orphan Annie,* with the daily secret code whispered to its listeners at the end of each program (which only Wiley could decipher with his special decoder mailed to him for sending in the label from a jar of Ovaltine) — these were the things that kept Wiley's interest. Billy and I read every book we could find about airplanes and the pilots who flew them.

We built a few store-bought model planes, but a dime was a lot of money in Depression days, and most of our models were made from black mud that grew the best cotton in Texas. Three days of heavy rain turned the black dirt into a thick gooey black paste that could grab and hold a wagon or automobile for a week, until warm sunshine loosened its grip. But that same black mud could be worked by hand and shaped into anything, just like clay. It was perfect for molding aircraft bodies, and wings and tails. We even shaped our propellers from mud. After the rain stopped, the sun would come out and the huge platform on the back of the gin was a perfect place to bake our models. They would harden into black pottery-like Spads, Fokkers, Nieuports, and Jennys.

This was a few years before pictures of World War II aircraft began to show up in Comic Books, Big Little Books, and all those places where farm kids could find pictures of airplanes. So we built models of nearly all the World War I stuff. The few books we had were filled with drawings of the Red Baron and Captain Eddie Rickenbacker, and of course there was Tailspin Tommy in near-real life when we had the chance to walk or drive the seven miles to the picture show in Mart.

We built low-wings and high-wings and biplanes and even the Red Baron's tri-wing Fokker. We never could find a way to color the Fokker red. Uncle John found us a can of red paint that had been left around the cotton gin for some reason, but the mud just soaked up the paint and all we had left to show for our effort was a trace of red-tinted glaze on black mud.

The real challenge came when we tried to fly the things. They were heavy, and the wings were thick and there was no power to turn the mud propellers. About the only thing the sad little models could do when we threw them off the top of the 20-feet-high platform was to dive straight down like a rock and smash into the hard ground below.

Later, when flying his last training flight, Billy's real-life P-40 would do the same thing with Billy inside. He was all excited about going to a P-51 squadron as soon as his last flight was completed. But for some reason, mid-way in the flight, Billy's P-40 exploded. It was probably caused by a faulty line or tank that slowly dripped gaso-line into some place where gasoline was not supposed to be. The fumes accumulated until they produced a ball of pressure looking for a spark. And then just the right kind came along, most likely a nice red-hot speck of metal, flicked out by a nearby engine exhaust. At any rate, what-ever it was that was needed, it all got together and pro-duced one hell of an explosion. What was left of Billy and his P-40 dropped like a rock and smashed into little bro-ken pieces. They could not be put together again. The desert ground in southern Arizona is just as hard as the ground had been below our launch platform in what was once upon a time a little community called Victoria.

With the roar of an aircraft engine slamming suddenly

to full power, the mid-morning routine of a late spring day was shattered. Across the small training field seasoned pilots and crewmen turned toward the sound. The Corsair was low — directly over the main gate of NAAS Corry, an auxiliary Navy training field near Pensacola, Florida. The left blue gull-wing was pointed straight down; the long nose was high. The explosion of noise somehow exemplified the desperation of a young pilot fighting to stay alive.

He was our classmate, Virgil Gillette. We had flown together for six months at Cabaniss, another Navy field near Corpus Christi, Texas. This first flight at Corry was the start of our training to land the F4U Corsair (a powerful, single-seat, long-nosed fighter) aboard an aircraft carrier. This fighter had been used with much success by Navy and Marine pilots in World War II.

Adrenaline-powered fear blocked Virgil's thoughts. Instinctive reaction controlled. He pressed with all the strength in his right leg against the right rudder pedal, trying to lift the left wing. His right hand held the control stick full back. His left hand clutched the throttle. With great force he jammed the short stubby lever hard against the stop-plate, but the left roll continued.

The large propeller turned furiously in the morning air. The short gull-wings were stalled, providing no lift. The spinning blades slowed the fall of the Corsair but accelerated the roll — the same as when a kid holds the propeller of a rubberband-powered model and watches the body spin.

The Corsair, still rolling, cleared the entrance shack at the main gate. Two young Marine guards stared straight up, their eyes wide. With an ear-splitting roar, the tip of the left wing of the blue fighter passed several feet above their heads. The guards cupped their hands tightly over their ears. The F4U continued toward the end of the runway.

As the F4U passed over the parking ramp just inside the fence, the left wing sliced another aircraft — an SNJ — neatly in half. The student pilot in the front part of the yellow trainer suddenly found himself with nothing but air behind him. His instructor, who was walking toward the aircraft from the hanger, stopped a good distance away and stared in shocked disbelief.

The Corsair managed to hang in the air. It continued to roll until totally inverted over the end of the runway. The canopy was locked open. Virgil's head, covered only with a cloth helmet and goggles, traveled at 100 miles an hour, 20 feet above the runway. The engine roared with full power. The huge propeller spun savagely and the nose of the Corsair began to drop.

The propeller dug into the concrete runway. Gasoline lines ruptured. Sparks ignited fumes. Instantly, the Corsair was a giant ball of volatile orange-red flame. A shock wave of heat crossed the field and black smoke from burning oil and gas began its climb into the spring morning. The Corsair, crushed inside the flame, continued to slide inverted down the concrete slab.

It took nearly two minutes for the fire truck to reach the crash and hit the flames with its powerful shower of white foam. When the fire was out, blackened metal stanchions outlined the fuselage. Parts of the blue wings remained. A massive crane rumbled forth from a near-by hanger and its large cables were attached to the plane. The skeleton fuselage was lifted.

From the cockpit, a smoking, blackened, charred human shape fell to the runway.

Just a few days before, some members of our flight had treated Virgil to a "mini" bachelor party. We had little time. The groom-to-be was scheduled to meet Charlotte that night so they could drive to Mobile to be married Saturday morning. All plans were without approval of the United States Navy. Student pilots who married before commissioning were immediately terminated from flight training. They were then sent to the fleet to serve as paint-chippers, or given some other exciting duty.

Virgil had met Charlotte in Corpus Christi. When our class went back to Pensacola for additional Corsair training, Charlotte went too. She rented a neat little apartment near the air station, where several from our class would stop by for talk and a cold beer at every opportunity. She and Virgil were a pleasure to be around. Charlotte worked as a waitress at a drive-in restaurant and did well with tips. She was a good-looking girl with a great sense of humor. Her smile was warm, quick, and natural. When she learned that she was pregnant, she and Virgil were married.

Her miscarriage happened two months after she and one of our classmates escorted Virgil's body back to Oregon.

Chapter 3

My Aunt Milly died not long after my Uncle John, and for a while they were like the words to a Kathy Mattea song. Two old people are in the same hospital on different floors, and one day they wheel the two into the same room and the husband strokes the fading thin hair of his sick wife. The old woman, who had not spoken a word in a long while, suddenly recognizes her husband of a lifetime. She smiles weakly, and then in a tiny, frail voice, she asks, "Where've you been?"

My Aunt Milly got better and lived a few more years, all in a nursing home, and after my Uncle John was gone I was able to go a few more times to Texas and visit with her. I sat on the side of her bed and we talked about the old days in Victoria. I looked into her eyes and saw the love that was still there, and the small, faint smile; and I hoped that she was able to see the same thing in mine. Finally, the subject of her son, Billy, came up. Although it had been more than 50 years since we had buried what was left of him in a little graveyard in Waco, she said, "Kenneth, it never gets any better. People used to try to tell me that time would heal and that I would slowly feel relief and that the hurting would stop, but people tell little lies sometimes, just to try and make others feel better, and I still do not know if people should do those kinds of things or not. I just know that they were lies and that, in the end, they did no good at all."

I looked into her eyes again, and I could still see the love and the little smile, and I could smell the salt-bacon frying in her old skillet and taste her hot biscuits covered with the best-tasting white gravy that ever was made on this earth (which she always said was God's), and I felt her strong thin arms around me, squeezing real hard when she had not seen me in a long time; and I knew all over again, if only for a moment, what life is all about, and how it was intended to be.

When Billy was killed, I was back in Hillsboro, living with my mother and her new husband, a nice man and hard worker named Porter Morelock. He was foreman of a line crew on the Katy railroad. I was beginning my last two years of high school. Mama and Porter had bought a little home on North Covington Street, a block from the old courthouse. I had been working in Ft. Worth with my father, who had become a machinist and worked in a plant where they made shells for the bigger guns used in World War II. I was working nights as an apprentice machinist, and trying to stay awake during classes at Pascal High School during the day. My training began at 8P.M., studying machinist math and blueprint reading until midnight, then running a lathe or drill press from midnight until dawn. After nearly a year of struggling with this schedule, it was obvious to everyone that either the job or school would have to go. Lucky for me, Mama and Porter talked me into coming to Hillsboro and finishing high school.

So I quit my job and the training. I moved in with Mama and Porter, transferred from Pascal High in Ft. Worth to Hillsboro High, and got a part-time job in Willie Crane's Tailor Shop pressing clothes, a skill I had learned at a little shop in Itasca while still a small kid. I was on my way.

I tried out for the football team, because Willie Crane had played football for Hillsboro and told me it would be good for me. Willie was blind, shot in the eyes with a shotgun by his best friend in a hunting accident that also damaged his legs. It had all happened when he was still a young man. By the time I went to work for Willie he was in his middle years and he moved around the shop while sitting in his little four-legged wooden chair. He used the chair as a walker. Although Willie was not a large man, his arms were huge and strong as steel from constantly picking up one leg of the chair, moving it forward, then picking up his weight on the other leg and repeating the movement over and over. All the time he seemed to know exactly where he was going without ever asking anyone to give him a hand.

Willie wore dark glasses, and when he talked, he tossed his head the way Ray Charles does when he's performing. Ray does it while singing and playing the piano, looking at the ceiling, or turning this way and that, searching for the eyes of his audience, which he is never able to see except in his mind. But Ray is blessed with a talent that does not require vision. He sees the hearts of his audience in a way that only he could know and he reaches them with the soul of his music.

Willie Crane did his talking and listening in the same way, both at the same time, making the same movements with his head; but Willie reached the soul of those who knew him, with nothing but the simple use of words — you could only sense the music. Simple, everyday words really, but they conveyed his thoughts with a depth of feeling that I have seldom encountered. And there was always the part that was unspoken, that sense of compassion that was always there. It could only have risen from the depths of ashes that were left from a type of suffering for which there are no words.

When Willie was not walking his chair around the shop, talking with us few workers, just casually checking that everything was O.K., he was in the front office talking with customers and old friends. He was married to a beautiful woman who came into the shop often. I never asked if they met before or after Willie was blinded in the accident. It was not important. They seemed to be crazy about each other.

My Aunt Lois, the youngest of my grandmother Atkinson's three children, was the first female All-State basketball player from Hill County. She grew up in Itasca, and was a very beautiful and popular girl. She told me that when she was young she double-dated with Willie and that he was a very handsome fellow and a great dancer. Since my Aunt Lois said so, it has to be true. She is one of the most honest and straight-talking women

I have ever known; and I would say those words even if she was not still living and just might read this one day.

So, because of Willie Crane I played football for Hillsboro High, and it was on the football field that I first met Gus Hilton. Gus lived just a few blocks away on South Covington. With all of my moving around, I had never played team sports in any sort of organized manner, and I was fortunate to have a friend like Gus Hilton to give me an occasional tip. He was one of the best all-round athletes ever bred, grown, and trained in Hill County.

Gus could run a hundred yards, with full football uniform on in the heat of a Texas August in close to 10 seconds. Playing right end, he could catch a football it if was thrown anywhere near as close as the next county. All Dexter Bassinger, our quarterback, or Bobby Dohoney, our pass-throwing halfback, had to do was get the ball over the head of the defensive safety and it was six points for Hillsboro. Gus liked nothing better than to see his picture in the paper, catching the winning touchdown while still high in the air, grinning wide for the camera, and at the same time looking back at the sad little safety whom he had just faked out of his jock-strap.

Gus could also handle the basketball and shoot it. He was the first player in Hill County to consistently shoot a one-handed jump shot, and also be able to score more than 20 points when needed in a critical game. He even shot his free throws with one hand, which in the early and mid-forties was sacrilegious.

But the true genius of Gus Hilton was his limp. At least that is what we thought at the time. On Friday nights during a football game, he would run like crazy all over the field with nothing but the smoothest flowing stride ever seen in Hill County. Then, on Saturday mornings after a game, he was a different Gus. All of us players would sit on the curb in front of Brown's Drug Store, across from the courthouse, just to watch Gus limp. And then of course there was the fact that nearly every girl in Hillsboro High, on a Saturday morning after a football game, would drive by Brown's just to grin, or maybe wave; and if one of us asked some of them to join us they would always reply, "No time now. Going shopping," or some such thing. And of course most of us had dates with some of them for that Saturday night and when we picked up our dates they would say, "I saw you sitting in front of Brown's." And we would reply, "Yeah," and that would be the end of that until the next ball game.

The show would start around nine o'clock in the morning when Gus would leave his house, head down a narrow street that went alongside the post office, and then carefully, watching traffic, cross over the busiest street in town. It was the highway that came down from Dallas and Ft. Worth and went right through the middle of downtown Hillsboro. It was called Waco Street because that was where it was headed, and Gus would cross there and then head on up the two blocks of sidewalk to Brown's. He would be limping all the way, and after he crossed over to the sidewalk he would look up to see how many of us were there.

Then we could see the smile begin. Watching Gus Hilton smile was like seeing a sudden shot of sunshine break through dark clouds on a cold rainy day. And when the smile began, Gus's limp would get downright professional. He would step with whichever leg was giving him the least trouble on that particular Saturday, and then drag the other one around like Chester did years later on TV's *Gunsmoke*. But no one had ever heard of TV in 1945, so with Gus it was all original. At the time we all thought the limp was just a good act, never sure if it was real or fake.

Then, finally, he would reach Brown's and one of us would casually look up and ask, like we had just noticed that he was there, "How's it going, Gus?" And the grin would give way for just a quick flash of serious expression, and he would reply, "O.K., I guess." And then we would make room for Gus on the curb, and he would sit, and we would talk a little about the game the night before, and wait for the next car with pretty girls to drive by.

January 1951 was a long time coming. We were all tired. Over a month at sea. Often two flights a day.

During the past 43 days, the carrier group had lost six pilots and twice as many planes. We had flown endless close-air support missions to assist in the successful evacuation of thousands of Army and Marine personnel trapped near the Chosin Reservoir. The Korean War, destined for more years, would end where it started, at the

38th parallel.

But that was ahead and out of sight. At the moment there was liberty. We were scheduled for a rest camp in the mountains of western Japan. Millpointer, Jake, Red and a half dozen others of us were first on the liberty boat.

Near the depot where we were to catch the train for the resort was a small Army Officers' Club. Each of us made a fast dash to the club to grab a bottle of booze. The soldier at the desk was neat, properly attired in freshly starched khaki, and he was young. Behind him were enough cases of various kinds of liquor to supply the entire Eighth Army.

"I am sorry, gentlemen," he said politely. "I can sell you all you want, a drink at a time over the bar. But no bottles!"

The soldier's words brought a stunned silence to our chattering little group. Hiding embarrassment, the shiny new corporal managed a fragile smile. He faced a blanket of cold, disbelieving stares and sensed the rage that would follow. Hastily he added, "There is a war on, you know!"

We missed the train, we missed lunch and we missed dinner. To be absolutely truthful, we did not eat at all. We drank double martinis at the bar. Throughout the afternoon we discussed most thoughtfully several problems in Korea as we saw them, particularly the importance in wartime for senior military personnel to assure fair distribution of critical supplies.

While our conversations continued, more of our buddies from the carrier drifted into the small club. By dark, the Army's secluded little sanctuary for officer relaxation was overcrowded. It was packed with disorderly drunken activity, both Army and Navy.

By 8P.M. the first fights started. By 11P.M. the club manager, an Army major, was found in the men's head — "Latrine!" countered the Army. Whatever they wanted to call it, the major was unconscious. A toilet seat was draped neatly around his neck. It was rumored that someone had caught him in the act of trying to set clocks ahead so that he could close the bar early. It was also reported that during the height of confusion, certain unthinking and non-disciplined Navy personnel "borrowed" the club's jeep.

Before midnight our congregation of Naval officers was ordered back to the ship. By morning, General MacArthur had restricted the entire crew of the USS Princeton to stay aboard ship for the remainder of our stay in port.

Mercifully, before the day was over, our Task Force Commander, Admiral Ofstie, was able to persuade MacArthur's staff to allow our group of tired and hungover warriors to depart the ship for rest camp. We were escorted aboard the train by armed Marines who managed to look serious when Army was around.

Dave Millpointer and I were too tall to stretch out in the small Japanese bunks. At 2A.M. we were sitting in the empty coach section of the train, talking the night away. Between verbalization of various worldly matters and thoughtful response thereto, we sipped from bottles that we had carefully sneaked from our safe aboard ship.

We were well into our discussions, and the bottles,

when we were joined by an Army colonel. He was fully dressed, both blouse and tie. His shiny eagles were easy to spot. His three campaign ribbons were topped by the good conduct medal from World War II.

The colonel introduced himself most proudly, and then asked, "May I join you, gentlemen?"

His deeply tanned face wore a constant smile and his gray sideburns added a touch of dignity to the occasion. His accent was New England, possibly Boston, at any rate positively grand. But all things considered, our new arrival rankled our meditative mood with an infusion of unwanted aloofness. Despite the warnings flashed to our most alert senses, Millpointer and myself, with our nods and mock toast, gave consent for the colonel to join us.

Our newly arrived guest then tersely refused our most generous offer of a drink from our private stock. He persisted even after we removed one of the bottles from its worn and soggy brown paper bag so that we could proudly show the label.

Then, with little preamble, and most certainly without solicitation, the uninvited colonel began a rather detailed colloquy of the Korean War. He professed to know facts and details that were highly secretive and exclusive to those with a need-to-know. He proceeded to engulf us with classified information not intended for the likes of ensigns. At times his voice hushed to a whisper, as though the seemingly empty coach car might have ears.

The colonel continued his discourse, and Millpointer and I listened for what seemed to be a very long period of time. I am proud to report from most reliable recall, that throughout our distress 'Pointer and I remained courteously attentive.

Only occasionally did we allow ourselves a small sip from our bottle. Even then we kept our eyes focused sharply on our speaker. After each genteel and succinct swallow we reassumed our expressions of concentration and hung onto the good colonel's every word.

We were, after all, officers and gentlemen. Like most young citizens of our generation, we had first been trained in matters of etiquette by our parents, then enrolled for additional training. We were honed and polished, with gentle persuasion, by seasoned Marine sergeants, into distinguished, attentive, polite, and by all means compliant, Navy Pre-Flight graduates.

Even so, Millpointer and I were near our tolerance level when the colonel finally made a mistake. He paused a few seconds too long in his seemingly endless dissertation. 'Pointer was able to insert a quick question.

"Colonel, what is your job?"

A quizzical expression crossed the colonel's face. "What do you do for the Army, Colonel?" 'Pointer repeated his question. He was careful to use his best midwestern drawl. (Millpointer's four Oconomowac, Wisconsin, brothers — veterans of World War II, one an Olympic-caliber skier, and all very good muskie fishermen — would have been proud of their little brother.)

The colonel's face brightened as he understood the question. "I am responsible for the entire Far Eastern schedule for the United States Army Band." There was a distinct note of pride in the colonel's voice.

Dave's face remained totally blank. His eyes were a vacant stare. "I am sorry, Colonel. I did not hear you."

Again 'Pointer's expressionless face.

"I am in charge of the Army Band," the colonel said.

Although his appearance reflected a fragile interest, 'Pointer remained quiet. Then he looked my way. His countenance indicated that we should be flattered to be in the presence of such magnificence.

Dave then leaned slowly towards the colonel until his face was not a foot away. He grinned a disguised sarcasm that only a few of us who knew him well could discern from warm friendship.

"Colonel," he said. "That is goddamned fascinating!"

The older man was silent; his agreeable demeanor remained unchanged. A few quiet moments passed while the colonel carefully analyzed 'Pointer's reply.

Finally, our guest's dignified expression beamed an even wider smile of satisfaction. The colonel was most definitely a man who appreciated proper respect.

A short time later 'Pointer and I were back in our short bunks. We lay flat on our backs, our knees bent as best we could inside the small cubical. What remained of our cherished private stock sloshed uncelebrated in small paper cups balanced on our stomachs.

When we last saw the good colonel, he was cautiously analyzing curious reflections as they masqueraded across his small, darkened coach window.

'Pointer and I resumed our exchange of thoughts concerning all the happenings of the last month or so. In regard to our most recent encounter in the club car, carefully chosen words expressed our very frank opinion concerning various human types who are allowed to roam freely across our planet and interrupt momentous occasions.

The rumble, clatter, rumble of the little narrow-gauge Japanese train continued its soothing and bumpy cadence. Lengthening periods of silence began to separate our deliberations. The last of our private stock was sipped slowly as all consciousness was gradually replaced by deep and untroubled slumber.

When we awoke, our bodies were refreshed. We were excited and most anxious to start our new day, determined to persevere in our search for rest and relaxation.

Chapter 4

Except for the times I spent with my Aunt Milly and Uncle John and my cousins Billy and Wiley, I was raised mostly by women. My father remarried and started another family when I was a teenager. Prior to that time he was cursed by many devils, and pulled in many directions by itches he was never able to scratch. He was a few years older than my mother and had been in the Navy for a short time, which ended when he was medically discharged after a painting-fume accident below decks — not an uncommon shipboard accident in the days when there was very little ventilation deep inside the hull of a large cruiser.

My father was 19 years old when he married my mother, and she was 16 years old when I was born — just two uneducated kids, who had no idea what they had gotten themselves into. They were separated before I was born and divorced shortly after.

Despite the whiskey, which then took control of my father's life, he managed to have a tour as a Texas Ranger, a newspaper reporter, a salesman, a lay preacher, and finally, a master machinist. He was called Hank, and there was not time for me to live enough years to obtain sufficient wisdom to truly understand the demons that pursued him until he was dead at 54.

I had a few visits with my father during his final illness, and I flew out from Florida at the end when I received my stepmother's call. I was hoping to be with him those last few hours, but I was too late. His lungs had been eaten away with cancer and surgery, and there was nothing left with which he could take just one last decent breath, only a final desperate gasp.

When my father remarried, he chose a wonderful woman named Jewel, who was from a very old and large Texas family. I therefore expected the sizable number of relatives who came for the funeral, but I was amazed at the number of Hank's old friends who came from all over. During the next few days nearly all of them got me aside at one time or another, just to let me know something extraordinary about the special father that I had lost. I am sure they did the same for my brother and sisters. Pop's remarriage brought into the world my half brother and three sisters who have become one of my life's very special pleasures.

I also spent unique time with another person at my father's funeral. In this instance it was not for some stranger to tell me something new about Hank, for I knew my father better than he did, even though the person was my grandfather — my father's father, George Atkinson. Until a short time before, no one in the family had seen Grandfather George for 50 years. Until that day I knew no facts, only rumors about my grandfather, little whispers here and there while I was growing up. About the time my father became seriously ill, my Aunt Milly managed to locate Grandpa in a small town in Missouri. Before the funeral Grandpa George and I escaped to a motel and spent the entire night talking, just the two of us.

From the turn of the century until he disappeared and started a new life in 1912, my grandfather had been a conductor on the Katy railroad. He and my grandmother, Myrtie Atkinson, lived in Hillsboro; and Grandpa George made about three round trips a month to St. Louis. Although he was away from home a lot, a conductor on the Katy in the early 1900s was a prestigious job. He made good money and had settled my grandmother and their three children into a nice home in Hillsboro.

My grandmother, Myrtie, had an identical twin sister named Byrtie, and before they died they set a record as the oldest living identical twins in the country; at least the oldest ever reported. Myrtie died a few weeks short of age 100 and Byrtie died four years later. They were two of the six daughters of a successful farmer in North Texas named Carter, who was the cousin of another Carter who settled in Georgia, and who had a great-grandson named Jimmy, who grew peanuts in Plains, Georgia, before becoming our 39th President.

Jimmy and I have never met and I do not know if he is aware of his Texas relatives. I knew little about the Carter side of the family until a recent visit with my Aunt Lois, when she presented me with a great old picture of the Carter family and told me the background. Although Jimmy and I were both in the Navy (him under water and me above it), I feel closer akin to him from his often quoted remark in a Playboy article in which he stated that he had sometimes "lusted in his heart." Those I know on the Texas side of the family concur that the Carters and the Atkinsons have at least one thing in common.

It would be difficult to explain George Atkinson without some knowledge of Myrtie Atkinson. In a way it would be easier to explain Myrtie if Jimmy Carter had been President three or four generations sooner. It would have given my grandmother a little more reason to carry off the role of a descendent from European royalty who no longer has money, only titles.

My grandfather called her Myrt. Her request to be called Mother Atkinson by her grandchildren came forth from the mouths of Billy and Wiley and myself, as "Ma Atchie." This she accepted, and this it remained by family members for most of her hundred years. When I was about four years old, I developed meningitis and diphtheria at the same time and was given up by the doctors as a hopeless case. The best they could offer was that if I should live I would be a lifelong cripple. It was Ma Atchie who helped my mother massage my legs for hours each day, and keep ice packs on my head and heat packs on my feet to draw the fever from my brain.

During the worst years of the Great Depression, when there was not even 50-cents-a-day work at the mill, my Ma Atchie decided that since we could not afford ice, she would sell her icebox for food money. The used-furniture man offered her 50 cents. My Ma Atchie told him, "Before I will give you that icebox for fifty cents, I'll let my grandson use it to learn how to take things apart," and that is what she did and I can still remember learning to handle a screwdriver, taking apart and putting together again Ma Atchie's icebox.

When Grandfather George and I had settled into the motel for the night before my father's funeral, he began the conversation by saying, "Well, Kenneth, I suppose you have heard stories all your life about me deserting my family."

He went on to say that he appreciated the opportunity to tell me what really happened so that I would know the facts. He also made it clear that he was not going to try to let himself off the hook.

"What I did was wrong. Bad wrong. My selfish act hurt an awful lot of people, including myself, and if I had it to do all over again, I would find another way. But the past is the past and there is no changing it."

He said that he had been on a long run to St. Louis and that he came home tired. He explained that my Ma Atchie was an obsessively jealous and proud woman and that she had been on his case for weeks. George said that as soon as he walked into the house she started up all over again.

"Hell! I couldn't take any more right then, so I left and went back to the depot and caught the next run to St. Louis."

My grandfather figured it would take a few days to make the trip, and that by the time he returned to Hillsboro, Myrt would have cooled off a little and he would try again. At least that was what he had in mind.

"But right before the train got back to St. Louis, one of my buddies came back and told me, 'George, your wife has the sheriff waiting for you. He has a warrant to arrest you for family desertion.' Well, Kenneth, that is when I made my stupid mistake. I just kept going."

George said that one thing led to another. At first he intended to come back every week, and then finally it was every year, and then, "Well hell! I just never did."

He wound up in Detroit, working in the automobile factories, and made a lot of money. He said that he sent a bunch of it to his brother in west Texas so he could get it to Myrt and the children in such a way that she could not track him down.

"Now I find out that my brother became a wealthy man and never sent Myrt a dime," he said. "It is a good thing the son-of-a-bitch is dead or the sheriff would be after me again."

In essence, that is what my grandfather told me over the course of a night of talking. He died not long after, and I have often speculated as to what would have happened to the Atkinson family in the course of a single generation, if one man had simply returned home to argue things out with his wife rather than disappear.

Each time I theorize about the subject, I always come to the realization that if my grandfather had returned, and if he and Myrt had been able to make their marriage work, my Pop would probably have finished high school and gone on to college. As a result, Hank would not have been distracted enough to marry a 15-year-old girl who was bewildered and confused because she had just lost her mother. And as a result of that, I would not be here and that is always the end of it. I have enjoyed my life far too much to speculate on having missed it. My wife has a firm conviction that whatever happens, happens for the best. I often tell her that every now and then she just happens to make sense.

The next day we buried Hank. Later, on the plane ride back to Pensacola, I had hours to think about my father. My earliest memory is of Pop in uniform, taking me into a high tower where people looked for forest fires. Then, I remember when I was at the gin in Victoria playing with Billy and Wiley, and Aunt Milly came out into the yard and handed me a letter from my father. It was one of the few letters I can remember getting from him, except during Korea when he wrote quite often. Inside the letter was a shiny new dime, and it seemed like all the money in the world. Billy and Wiley were as excited as I was and we immediately headed for the little store at the crossroads. Our favorite thing from the store was an "all-day sucker." It was a large block of caramel on a stick, and if you nursed it slowly it would indeed last nearly all day. All-day suckers were a nickel, but somehow on that special day, we talked the owner of the store into selling us three for a dime.

The last time I saw Billy, when he was headed for Sheppard Field in Wichita Falls to begin his Army Air Corps training, we were joking about all-day suckers. Billy said that he would mail me one if they had them in the PX, but his mind was soon on other matters. The Army Air Corps was a busy place in 1943.

Far more important than the dime, the best thing my father ever did for me was to recognize that I was a physical coward and that I was walking away from fights. He bought me my first set of boxing gloves. They were 16 ounces of beautiful purple leather with gold trim, and they were to become an important part of my life. All that Hank said to me when he gave me the gloves was, "Learn to use these. They will help you."

I practiced with a few friends in private and learned the fundamentals, but during all of my high school days I avoided fistfights. This was hard to do, and oftentimes a foolish thing to do on a football field, or in a schoolyard. It can leave you with a sick feeling in the pit of your stomach. My "coward cure" was to come from Gus Hilton later, when we went off to college.

Tom Dreis was a man glad to be alive. He always had a smile and a cheerful remark to make you feel good. The fact that Tom lived through World War II was due to his skill as a pilot and to the generous blessings of the fickle finger, but credit is also due a Navy Admiral who had guts. It is also due to his thoughtfulness and optimistic attitude — just the nature of Tom Dreis.

The admiral's part began on the afternoon of a tense day in the Western Pacific in June 1944. A Navy patrol plane spotted elements of the Japanese fleet. Tom and many other Navy pilots were launched from carriers to attack. Distance to the target and the need to land the returning aircraft before dark were matters set aside. The important thing was to hit the target immediately. Tom did two significant things that day. He made it to the target where his bombs were instrumental in sinking a Japanese aircraft carrier. For this achievement he was awarded the Navy Cross. Next, thanks to an admiral who ordered lights to be turned on in the middle of a war zone, Tom was able to fly his aircraft safely aboard a small jeep carrier, although he had no training for night landings. For this bit of skill, guts, and daring, he was given extra shots of brandy.

I met Tom Dreis later, in 1951. Red Rumble and I returned from a tour in Korea with VA-195 and were transferred to VA-65 for a quick turnaround. Tom was one of the recalled World War II reserves assigned to VA-65. He was new to the AD and curious about Korea. I was able to give him a few tips on flying the Skyraider and what to expect later. He told good World War II stories, Australia and all, and he was damned interesting to follow on liberty — the only man I have ever known who consistently received notes from good-looking women in strange bars. Needless to say, I enjoyed tagging along when we were on the beach.

When we got to Korea, things had changed. During the first cruise we often went in low. There was anti-aircraft fire, but we were able to work around it for close air support and other low-level work. Now, just a few months later, the intensity and accuracy of North Korean AA fire had improved dramatically. By the end of 1951 new technology given to the North Koreans by the Russians and the Chinese made air strikes against hardened targets damned dangerous.

A direct hit from high altitude flack blew one of our ADs out of the air on our squadron's very first flight. This occurred even though we came onto target at 13,000 feet and rolled in for only one steep dive. Such tactics were totally different from the low-level racetrack patterns that were routine during the earlier part of the war.

After the flight and debrief, Tom joined several of us younger pilots who were nursing a medicinal brandy in the ready-room.

"Tom, was that anything like the Big One?" I asked, referring of course to his experiences in World War II.

"Child's play!" was his quick reply.

During the next several months, beginning in January 1952, VA-65 pilots flew a lot of combat. Now and then our carrier stopped for what the Navy calls R and R — Relaxation and Recreation. Tom and I made several liberties together.

About midway during the cruise, Robert Pierpoint, a CBS correspondent working for Edward R. Murrow, came aboard to do a story about a particular bomb that had been tracked from its point of manufacture to Tom Dreis's AD. Tom and some of the squadron were featured on one of Murrow's prime time TV shows.

On our next shore leave, Pierpoint invited Tom and me to spend a few days at the Tokyo Press Club. This was a good deal. We stayed in Bob's quarters, drank champagne for breakfast and met a lot of interesting people.

One who often stayed at the Club was Maggie Higgins, a highly qualified and well-known Korean War correspondent. Maggie was young and extremely attractive. Rumors flourished that she got her best stories by sharing a sleeping bag with the fighting troops. Someone told Tom and me that Maggie, after a few drinks, did not hesitate to confirm the story.

"I did, honey! Two bodies are warmer than one. It was 30 degrees below zero. The wind often hit 50 miles an hour and was a constant howling terror. The combined wind-chill factor was so low you did not want to know the numbers. Throughout the long nights the Chinese blew their squeaky little trumpets and shouted, 'Yanks, you die.' And then they came. Time and time again. After each charge, we stacked more bodies, soon to become frozen and serve as sand bags to reinforce our meager protection.

"Now, in the middle of all that hell, if you can imagine anything happening besides trying desperately to get a little sleep and praying to stay alive, then Honey, you were not there."

Back with the squadron we found the war had become even more intense. Each strike called for careful planning to avoid heavy losses. Tom and I flew together only on large strikes requiring more than one division. He was a division leader and I usually flew the section for Art Downing, our Air Group Commander.

After every flight on which Tom and I were in the air at the same time, I would ask, "Was that like the Big One?"

Each time the same reply, "Child's play!"

Then, on June 23, 1952, we flew the first of several air strikes to knock out North Korea's hydroelectric system, the major source of power for North Korea and Southern Manchuria. The first target was Suhio, a large power station on the Yalu River near the West Coast of Korea. Just across the river a few miles to the west was Antung airfield, a safe Manchurian sanctuary for Russian MiGs. On a regular basis during this part of the war, Air Force jets would fly north on the West Coast of Korea towards the Yalu. MiGs would launch from Antung and air-to-air combat would commence. Taking advantage of this routine, the Navy and Air Force planned a joint operation.

Art Downing, our Carrier Air Group Commander, a command still called CAG, was selected to lead a three-carrier strike force, the largest Navy air strike since World War II. I flew Art's section. Tom Dreis led the third division. Behind Tom were six more four-plane divisions of ADs from the other carriers. Jets from the three air groups flew high cover.

Art Downing was a "pilot's pilot," a well-worn phrase, but in Art's case it fit perfectly. During World War II he became one of the Navy's most decorated flyers. His SB2C dive-bomber hangs today in the Naval Air Museum in Pensacola. I once talked with a chief who worked in the boiler room of one of our carriers during World War II. Art was then a junior officer new to combat and came to the chief wanting to know all about Japanese carriers. He was not concerned with getting a hit, Art wanted to know which smokestack on which carrier to put his bomb so as to achieve the most damage. He then went out and did exactly what the chief told him to do.

The night before the strike on Suhio, Art and his staff worked late into the night compiling and analyzing information necessary to make the mission a success. I listened for a long time. They were still at it when I turned in.

The plan was to rendezvous three air groups from three carriers off the east cost of North Korea, fly across mountainous terrain at tree-top level, and arrive over Suhio on the second that the MiGs were engaging the Air Force's F-86 Sabres. If we were too early, or too late, we would be sitting ducks.

The next morning we launched. We rendezvoused; we flew at treetop level. Just as we began our fast climb to 10,000 feet, I heard the chatter of F-86 pilots preparing to engage the MiGs. It was the only time I ever heard air-to-air combat talk except in movies. I was intrigued. The real thing sounds just like Hollywood.

As we started our climb, I could see for the first time that Art had us right on the money. We reached 10,000 feet at the precise roll-in point and exactly on time. Art called, "Zero Zero Buzz-saw rolling in!"

I looked at my watch. The second hand was passing zero.

We were loaded with two 2000- and one 1000-pound bombs. Red Rumble was flying Tom Dreis's number-four position. He carried a large camera on one station rather than a bomb. Several of the major newsmagazines used a picture taken by Red's camera in their stories reporting the destruction of North Korea's hydroelectric plants. The photograph showed what looked to be near total destruction of the main facility.

Aboard the carrier, studying a blow-up of the photograph that was printed, we could see two ADs still in their dive. When the picture was snapped, less than one-third of the total strike force had dropped their bombs. I have often speculated about the absolute chaos that must have existed at Suhio during the strike and after the bombs stopped.

As Art and I rolled in, black puffs from high-altitude flack were beginning to burst nearby. White puffs from low-altitude fire tracked us down. After pullout, Art stayed low, in the middle of the Yalu, with everything forward, going as fast as we could go. Within a few miles we lost all signs of enemy fire, which arched towards us from both sides of the river. Then Art gave our join-up signal and we headed for the carrier.

As the flights behind us began their runs, the flak became more accurate. A few aircraft were hit.

After the debrief, Tom, Red and I, and others got together for our usual brandy. By the second drink our adrenaline flow had dropped toward normal. The constant chatter of excited voices began to slow. Verbally we had re-flown every detail of the strike, from takeoff to who caught what wire on landing. I had managed to tell the group more than once about the second hand of my watch passing zero the moment CAG called "Rolling in!"

Finally, there was a lengthy silence. I caught Tom's eye.

"Well, Tom, was that one anything like The Big One?"

Although looking my way, Tom's mind was elsewhere. He took a moment to collect his thoughts before answering. Red and the others were quiet, looking at Tom.

Finally the old grin appeared. Tom looked at each of us. He took a moment to study our faces. Not one of us in the group, except Tom, had been in combat in World War II.

"Fellows, you have finally seen one like The Big One. That was one hell of a good show."

I think all of us younger pilots enjoyed the next brandy the best of all.

Years later I was reading details of carrier wars in the Pacific during World War II. On occasion we lost as many as 150 aircraft and their crews in a single day.

Suddenly, I could see again Tom Dreis's vacant stare during that brief moment after Suhio. Only a few of our aircraft had been hit. I remembered the split-second hesitation before he told us younger pilots exactly what we wanted to hear.

Tom Dreis was a man glad to be alive. He was also a genius with words that made your day.

Chapter 5

Janice Sanders was a year older than Gus and me. She was a cheerleader and one of the prettiest and most popular girls in Hill County. We started dating right after I started playing football. For some reason she saw something in me that only Gus and Dexter Bassinger, and Dexter's girlfriend Eulayne Keeton saw. There were a few others, like Red Duke, who became a famous doctor in Texas, and Bobby Dohoney, who retired as the old Hill County Judge, and Cecil Stubblefield, who, it is rumored, now owns most of the county. But the three of them lived on the Country Club side of town and ran in a different circle than Gus and I. Nevertheless, all of them went out of their way to be friendly to a shy and introverted mess of a kid who was not much of a ball player, but who tried hard, and who made good grades in school without trying hard.

Not long after I met Janice, I bought a Model-A Ford. I had saved enough to make a down payment, and Willie Crane signed to guarantee my note at the bank. The car was a 1929 coupe. My training in mechanics came in handy. I turned the trunk lid around, put in seats, and just like that I had a coupe with a neat little rumble seat. I rebuilt the engine and painted and polished the body until it was Henry Ford's original black.

For nearly two years it took Janice and myself and Gus and Maxine, and oftentimes Deck and Eulayne, all over Hill County. They were good years. Janice's, Maxine's, and Eulayne's popularity, Gus's and Deck's athletic ability, and Gus's grin, got us invitations to many social functions. By 1945 I was no longer the shy kid who fell asleep at his desk in Ft. Worth's Pascal High School.

And then I pulled a "Grandpa George" and made a stupid mistake. I fell head-over-heels in love with Janice Sander's cousin, Suzie Johnson. In looking back, falling in love with Suzie was not my big mistake. Hell, falling head-over-heels in love with a tall, thin, good-looking blonde with a Lauren Bacall sexy voice and great one-liners is what makes the world go around. But I should have been more honest with Janice.

I tried to play both sides of the street; and Suzie, who was not about to be in love with me, soon married an ex-Navy pilot returned from World War II.

Janice disappeared from my life as quickly as she had entered it. I do not remember that I ever said so much as goodbye. And that bothers me, because Janice Sanders was largely responsible for two very good and important years in my life. It is a little late, but "Thank you, Janice."

In the late fall of 1945, an ex-Navy flyer named Dumas landed a small aircraft in a wheat field outside Hillsboro.

Somehow Dumas had gotten first in line for a discharge when World War II ended. He then used his savings to buy a little Taylorcraft to barnstorm and give flying lessons. Gus and Deck and several of us got the word and drove the Model-A out to the field to take a ride.

Within a few weeks, right after football season ended, I sold my Model-A to continue taking flying lessons. When the car money was gone and I had soloed, Dumas told me I should find a way to join the Navy's flight program.

Several of us ball players could have graduated in June of '45, but we purposely missed a few credits so we could stay over and play football. World War II was about over and we were too young for the draft; at the time it made sense. After football season in the fall of 1945, high school was essentially over for some of us. We went to a few classes and sort of coasted, waiting to go through the formality of graduation in June of '46. So when Dumas told me about the Navy flight program, I was ready. What he did not tell me was that at the time, the Navy and all the other services were discharging hundreds of thousands, a lot of them pilots. All he said was, "Find a way."

I went to the Navy recruiting office in Waco and got there about lunchtime. There were two sailors in the office and they got a big kick out of a high school kid thinking he could just walk in and start flight training. Finally they told me that if I was that determined to try the Army Air Corps.

The Army was no different. They did try their best to sign me up for a hitch. No doubt Army recruiters had a quota to fill even in December 1945. They assured me that after basic training I could apply for flight training.

But I had already been warned about that scenario.

My thought was that if I were going into the service with no guarantee for flight training, I might as well go into the Navy right off. Somehow the ocean appealed to me more than trenches.

So I resigned myself to the thought of just being a sailor and doing my four years, and then using the G.I. Bill to go to college. However, when I reentered the Navy office, the Chief had gotten back from lunch and the two sailors had already briefed him about the young prospect, who would probably be back when he found out that he could not fly for the Army.

The Chief asked me into his office and I could see that he had been going through a stack of papers on his desk. In the stack of mostly useless verbiage he had located what turned out to be an early announcement concerning the Navy's Holloway Program.

Thankfully for mankind, there are always thinkers hiding in the wings, and, when the war ended, one of these analytical types did the Navy a great service. He was an Admiral named Holloway, who realized that neither the public nor Congress would be excited about funding millions of dollars for the training of future aviators when the Navy already had thousands of pilots they could not use.

Admiral Holloway began his search for cracks in the system. He found one in the methods used for funding the Naval Academy. There was not the first hint in late 1945 that public opinion still did not support the concept of a Naval Academy and its midshipmen. Holloway's thought was that if we train midshipmen to sail ships, why not train a special breed of midshipmen to fly airplanes? With this single thought in mind, Admiral Holloway found money for training new pilots at a time in our country's history when there was none. Time would prove him to be a very wise man. When the Korean War began, just five years later, the Navy had about 3,000 "Flying Midshipmen" wearing gold wings.

So the Chief gave me some exams and then sent me to Houston for more. When I got there I had an abscessed tooth that was killing me, but a Navy nurse took pity and kept me supplied with ice water to hold in my mouth for the day-long tests. There were about 40 of us being examined that day, and when I learned that I was one of only two selected, the pain from the tooth was not nearly so bad. All night, on the train ride back to Hillsboro, I was so excited I could hardly feel anything. I kept thinking about Billy and how we had always told each other that we would both be military pilots. Now Billy was dead, and after my experience with the recruiting offices I had about given up hope. But here I was, on my way to becoming a Navy pilot.

When I got back to Hillsboro, I could not wait to tell Gus. He had paid for one airplane ride with Dumas, and after the flight he had not seemed at all impressed. Therefore, I had not given the first thought to the idea that Gus might also want to be a Navy pilot. But when I finished telling him all about my adventure, Gus said, "Damn, that sounds like a great idea."

I had not told him about the Navy only selecting two out of 40. I knew that Gus was smart and had no problems with school, but he was more interested in people than books. Other than the one flight with Dumas, he had never shown interest in flying. So I thought to myself, O.K., Gus. Just go on down to Houston. There's nothing to it.

In two weeks he was back, grinning from ear to ear. "Damn, Ack Ack!" (a nick-name Gus had tagged me with when I first got to Hillsboro), "You didn't tell me they only took two out of 40. They had me sweating there for a while."

And then he told me that in March the two of us would be going to Southwestern University in Georgetown, Texas, as part of the early recruits for the Navy's Holloway Program.

For many years I have considered the odds that out of 80 young and healthy Texas kids, two of the four chosen for Navy flight training, at a time when selection was very competitive, would be from Hillsboro, Texas. In World War II, Hillsboro was a town of 10,000, with one grammar school, one high school, and one Junior College. They were all in a row in three ordinary and nearly identical buildings, but they were blessed with what must have been some of the most dedicated and outstanding teachers in the whole magnanimous state of glorious Texas.

Two of our pilots, Dale Faler and Dick Rowe, would be caught in flak bursts from the same target. Dick Rowe was hit as they approached their target and went straight in. His AD crashed in the middle of Hamhung, a sister city of Hungnam on the east cost of North Korea, 60 miles south of the Chosin reservoir. This was the area where thousands of Marines and Army personnel had been evacuated more than a year before.

Dale Faler was hit after he dropped his bombs and during pull-up. The two aircraft were hit so near the same time that a report back to the ship stated both planes were shot down with one flack burst.

("Hell No!" said Dale Faler, when I saw him recently for the first time since Korea. "We made the so and so's use two shells.")

Dale had bailed out low. His AD lost a wing and was spinning so violently that Dale passed out for a few seconds. When he regained consciousness, he was very low to the ground and said to himself, "Well, Dale, I guess we are going to die," and then immediately thought, "To hell with that!"

He put his feet on the seat of the AD and pushed as hard as he could. The next thing he knew he was in the air. He could not find his ripcord handle because it had fallen from its holder. Then he saw a sparkle in front of his eyes. It was the glare of sunlight reflecting from a metal ring, which was floating and spinning in front of his face. Dale grabbed the silver ring and pulled it. The chute blossomed, and Dale Faler landed softly on the edge of a bomb crater in the center of what was once a building in downtown Hamhung.

He said that his fall was arrested so suddenly that he touched the ground like he was stepping off the curb onto the street in front of his home.

When Dale told me this story, we were sitting over

drinks at my son's restaurant on Pensacola Beach. My eyes must have gotten a little glazed, as though I was dubious of the facts. Dale went on to explain that if you ever watch movies of parachute jumps, you can see that at the exact moment the canopy becomes fully open, the nylon cords attached to the harness will stretch several feet; an instant later they pop back.

When Dale's feet touched the ground, his parachute cords were pulling him upwards as fast as he was falling. Dale touched down as light as a feather. North Korean soldiers rescued him from a mob of angry civilians. In time, he wound up in a prisoner of war camp near the Yalu River.

Aboard ship, Dale had been the squadron comic. He was short and athletic and was often seen hanging from metal bars that supported the stack of bunks in "Boy's Town," the name given to junior ensign quarters. Dale would hang by one arm, scratch with his free hand, and make monkey sounds. It was therefore natural that when we heard "germ warfare" stories emanate from Dale's prison, which told of handkerchief parachutes tied to dead mice hanging in trees, Dale Faler would be the culprit. When I asked Dale about this, he said "No, that was another guy." But a gleam in Dale's eye told me there was more to the story than that.

John Koelsch, our helicopter pilot from the Princeton cruise, was also in a prisoner of war camp near Dale Faler. John would die there from torture and Koelsch's family, instead of being able to hear John laughing in the kitchen, would have his Medal of Honor to display proudly on their mantel. That is the way it happens sometimes, and in John's case that is the way it would remain. The medal was for John's bravery during the action that led to his capture, but it was also awarded because Koelsch was an example of honor for other prisoners.

Although Dale Faler did not mention the subject, he, too, suffered the horrors described most vividly in books written by fellow survivors. The only reference made by Dale concerning his treatment in prison was that he and a few others were not released until three months after the majority of the prisoners were back home. When I asked why, Dale just grinned and said, "They did not like me."

There is nothing special on Dale Faler's mantel except pictures of his kids, all born after Korea, and all destined to grow to adulthood, produce grandchildren, and do all those good things that life is all about.

While a prisoner of the North Koreans, Dale Faler suffered some of the worst horrors imaginable, but somehow he retained his sense of humor. He remained a natural comic. He stayed loose and saved the lives of other prisoners by simply giving our guys something to laugh about.

After the war Dale remained in the Navy. Following his retirement he became mayor of his hometown, Independence, Kansas. Until Dale told me of the mayor bit, I had never placed him and Harry Truman in the same cluster of brain cells. But the more I think about Independence, Missouri, and Independence, Kansas, the better I like the match. Somehow the towns and the men they produced seem to fit.

Chapter 6

In March of 1946, Gus Hilton and I enrolled in the oldest University in Texas — Southwestern University in Georgetown — a collection of beautiful old buildings bustling with over 700 students.

We were sworn in as apprentice seamen, Navy V-5, and fitted with World War II uniforms. They came complete with bell bottoms and white sailor hats, just like those worn by Frank Sinatra and Fred Astaire in World War II movies — the kind that were supposed to bring whistles of admiration from pretty girls.

We were then assigned rooms. They were in the "Navy Dorm," which was by far the finest dormitory on campus — an aged brick structure, which before the war had housed only pretty young females. At the beginning of World War II the building was confiscated from the daughters of prominent Texans by the Navy Department and made available for various Navy college programs.

In March 1946, World War II was over and high on the public's "to be forgotten" list. Prestigious Texas mothers wanted their daughters back in the "nice dorm," not the dilapidated wooden structure they had been forced into during the war.

In addition, the male civilian students, who included many returning veterans attending college on the GI Bill, resented new recruits who had never been "shot at with malice" receiving tuition and expense money that nearly matched that received by those who had.

So all of us in That Navy Group, soon learned to expect whistles when we walked across campus, now and then from pretty girls who felt secure that their mothers would never find out, but more often from surly warriors.

However, like most other happenings in life, our days slowly settled into routine and we V-5ers learned to cope. We were rolled out early, ate Navy chow, and did morning exercises and marching until our first class. During the day we were on a schedule similar to that of other students. In the afternoon after classes, Navy routine started anew — marching, military courses, and intramural sports.

Gus and I joined a football group, which played against various fraternities and other campus teams. One of our roommates, Dave Medley, a V-5er like us, was the son of Southwestern's coach. Dave was a very good athlete and quickly had his father recruit Gus for varsity basketball and both of us for football. I wound up at my old high school left-tackle position, playing football for Southwestern. I was blocked aside and watched as running backs from some of the finest college and military service teams in the Southwest scored touchdowns running weak-side plays against Southwestern. At the time it was upsetting, but I can see now that it was good training for young men who aspired to be junior officers.

However, what I remember best about Southwestern is my "coward cure" lesson from Gus Hilton. It all began after we had settled into Navy routine for about a month or so, and Gus and I, and Dave Medley and another roommate from El Paso (whose name has escaped me) were in our room for the usual study period following the evening meal.

We were all reading and trying to concentrate, and all was quiet except for the noise of Gus eating an apple. For over two years we had spent a lot of time together with hardly a cross word, but all of a sudden Gus's chomping irritated the hell out of me. I turned and glared.

"How about eating that damned apple someplace else. We are trying to study in here."

My sudden explosion shocked Gus as much as it surprised me, but my words of anger were out and there was no dragging them back. During the moment of silence that followed, I could feel our roommates turning to catch what was going on.

Then Gus gave me his answer. "Why in the hell don't you make me?"

There was more silence. I did not have to look to know that Gus and our roommates had me in focus, waiting for my reply.

I gave my usual rejoinder to any remark that would lead to a fistfight, "Oh don't start that stuff!"

"A good old Ack Ack response," said Gus. He glared my way and chomped even harder on the apple.

I shuffled some papers and made an attempt to appear as though I was concentrating on my studies. Dave and our other roommate did the same. Gus slowly resumed his own reading but made a point of enjoying his apple.

It was not over and I knew it, but following my established routine, I just ignored the incident and hoped the matter would somehow disappear. Such nonsense.

The whole thing did go away — until liberty that weekend. Not another word was said regarding our little spat, and all of us continued as if nothing had happened. Then, on Saturday night, Gus and I teamed up with two other students and headed for Austin.

Our coach in high school, Pug Galiga, had stressed to his players that good athletes did not smoke and they did not drink; to do so was to let your teammates down, and anyone caught not caring for the team's welfare would be better off elsewhere. A nice way of saying, "Drink alcohol and you do not play football for Hillsboro High."

When we got to Austin, the four of us chipped in and bought a bottle of whiskey. The alcohol hit us like bricks, and despite our preoccupation with finding bars with pretty girls who wanted to dance, it was not long before the subject of apple chomping came up. During the drive back to Georgetown, Gus and I began to shout at each other so loud that the driver stopped the car and told us to get out and settle our dispute. He and his buddy were tired of listening.

There was nothing to do but crawl out of the car. Gus was very drunk and I was just sober enough to dodge his wild swings, which began immediately. My leather soles were slipping on the gravel alongside the highway and all I could think about was just trying to keep Gus from landing a punch. He was swinging hard enough to knock

AD from VA-195, USS Princeton, receives launch signal for Close Air Support strike, February 1951.

*Tex "Ack Ack"
Atkinson and Janice
Sanders, Hillsboro,
Texas, 1945.*

*George Vaughn "Gus"
Hilton, 1945. One of the
best athletes ever in Hill
County.*

*"Brown's Corner," 1945.
Dexter Bassinger (stand-
ing), Douglas Conway (r.),
B.J. Barnes.*

Artist Blair Arnold's drawing of 100 year old Hill County Court House, Hillsboro, Texas.

Bob Finley (l.) and Tex Atkinson, after buying "Perpetual Motion," the Chevrolet that would not give up, Pensacola, 1948.

Ensign Hugo Scarsheim, USS Princeton, Korea, December 1950.
"Mayday! Mayday! I'm On Fire! I'm On Fire!" His final words
and the battle of the Chosin Reservoir are just memories now.

"Gootch" Johnson (l.), and Tom Dreis, VA-65, USS Boxer, June 1952.

*"Red" Rumble, VA-65, Room 117, USS Boxer, 1952.
Our home away from home.*

*Annie Atkinson, Dave Millpointer, and Red Rumble relaxing,
September 1950.*

VF-63 F4U Corsair is readied for catapult launch,
USS Boxer, Korea, 1952.

VA-65 Skyraider begins take off run aboard the USS Boxer, Korea,
1952.

George Elmies, Photo Pilot, mans his F9F Panther to record strike damage by Corsairs and ADs flying from the USS Princeton, May 1, 1951.

Suhio, June 23, 1952. 36 AD Skyraiders, from three carriers, dive bomb the largest of North Korea's hydroelectric plants.

VA-65 and Air Group Two pilots, USS Boxer, 1952, are led to the flight deck by Art Downing (extreme left).

*A bomb drops from an AD piloted by Gene Sizemore, VA-195, during landing aboard USS Princeton, May 1951. All attempts to release the bomb over target area and at sea failed.
The bomb did not explode.*

AD loaded for Close Air Support taxies into take off position, USS Princeton, Korea, 1951.

"Tiger Division," June 1951. (l. to r.) Dave Davidson, Dave Millpointer, Annie Atkinson, Tex Atkinson, Jake Jacobson.

Tom Dreis, Ready Room, USS Boxer, Korea, 1952.

VA-195 pilots aboard the USS Princeton, spring 1951.
(Kneeling, l. to r.)
J.B Whitmore, Carl Rochester, Don Monday, Jake Jacobson, Tex Atkinson, Carl Austin, David Davidson.
(Standing, l. to r.) Gene Sizemore, Wayne Irvin, Donald Scalla, Bob Stammerjohn, Ed Phillips, Red Rumble (front), Marv Quaid (behind), Sandy Sanderson (far back), Bob Notz (behind), Don Sparks (front), Bob Bennett, Dick Fouchet, Don Van Slooten (back), Nels Gunderson, Jack Everling, Swede Carlson.

Carlson's Canyon, Korea, 1951. Later to become known as The Bridges at Toko-ri in Michener's book and the movie.

A typical North Korean railroad bridge target. 17 feet wide and a 100 feet high, they were difficult to hit.

(l. to r.) Dick Rowe, Larry Pinzel, Russ Novak, and Dale Faler, VA-65, USS Boxer, spring of 1952, shortly before Dick Rowe and Dale Faler were shot down.

The much admired Rear Admiral Ralph Ofstie (center) leads the way.

Four unidentified officers search the sky during flight operations aboard the USS Boxer, Korea, 1952.

Explosions rock Hungnam waterfront on December 24, 1950. The last of the Marine and Army Chosin Reservoir survivors were safely aboard ships.

*Ken Wallace,
Blue Angels,
1964.
One of the
Navy's best,
and a true Jet
pioneer.*

*Directors Lounge, Flight Deck Control, USS Essex, 1956. An
authentic depiction of off-duty flight deck directors precisely illus-
trates the true character of the Flight Deck Chief.*

Carl Austin, VA-195, inspects special bomb that he later dropped on North Korea. USS Princeton, Korea, 1951.

me all the way back to Austin. I managed to stay on my feet, block his blows, and never took a single swing. Finally Gus ran out of steam. Our two buddies dragged us back into the car and we headed for Georgetown.

When we got to our room it was close to midnight, and Dave Medley and our El Paso roommate were snoring away. Gus was talking fast and loud, saying what a yellow so and so I was and how embarrassing it was for him to be buddies with someone who wouldn't fight. I ignored him and kept busy trying to get my uniform off. Anyone who ever wore a sailor suit knows that they are difficult enough to get out of when you are sober, but they are nearly impossible when you are drunk!

I finally got the blouse pulled over my head and thrown aside and concentrated on the bell-bottoms. I had to take my shoes off, and then about the time I got the pants down around my ankles, here comes Gus. He did not say a word but just waited until I was looking at him. Then he hit me as hard as he could. The blow caught me on the side of the face and I would still be flying backwards except for a closet door that stopped my fall.

Suddenly I was filled with a rage like I had never known before. The pure injustice of the thing filled me with wild fury. During our roadside scuffle I had not thrown one punch at Gus, then he waited until I could not move and knocked my head off.

I bounced off the door and yanked one leg free of the bell-bottoms. Then I led with a short left jab. When Gus went for it, I caught him square on the jaw with as good a right as I have ever thrown. Gus was drunk and he was limp, and the blow knocked him all the way across the room. He landed across Dave Medley's bed.

By this time our roommates were waking and Dave said something like, "What the hell is going on?"

Gus raised himself from the bed, rubbed his chin with one hand, and then his face brightened with a captivating grin. It was identical to the one he used on Saturday mornings in Hillsboro when he limped towards Brown's Drug Store.

Gus looked at Dave and El Paso. "What's going on is that Atkinson finally threw a punch."

Then Gus walked across to me, held up his hands so I would know that there would be no more fighting and said, "Peace Old Buddy. Let's get some sleep."

The next year and a half went quickly. I discovered that there was a flying club at a nearby airfield which was no longer used by the military. A newly discharged Army Air Corps pilot had a few small aircraft there and was renting the planes and giving lessons. I could not wait to start flying again and get my private license. This required about 50 hours of flight time, most of it solo, and the temptation to take a buddy for a flight before it was legal to do so was just too much.

I arranged to land at a field outside of Georgetown and pick Gus up for a ride. I landed the little two-seat Aeronca Champion without trouble. Gus got in and I taxied into position for take off. The deserted pasture had been mowed at some time in the distant past, but since then, weeds had grown a foot tall. When I started my takeoff run, grass wrapped itself around the wheels and axle, and I had to try three times before I finally got us airborne. Gus was in the back seat talking away, enjoying a special exhilaration that comes to the young when breaking rules.

We flew around the area for quite a while and Gus seemed to be excited about being in the air. The landing was no problem. I got out of the front seat and helped Gus out of the back. I then noticed that he had not buckled his seat belt. This disturbed me because I realized that in my rush to get in the air I had forgotten to take the time to make sure that Gus was properly strapped in. But the flight was over and no harm was done, so I simply made a mental note not to forget again. I then returned the Aeronca to the airport and met Gus back at school.

That night we were describing our escapade to some of our buddies and one of them told us that just a few months before, two guys had done exactly the same thing, except that the grass had wrapped around the wheels solid and the aircraft was flipped onto its back. Like Gus, the fellow in the back had not fastened his safety belt and was thrown through the top of the aircraft and killed. There were no further passenger flights until I got my private license.

After the summer semester was over, the Navy's contract with Southwestern ended. The girls got their dormitory back for the fall semester, and us V-5ers took off our sailor uniforms and mingled with the civilian students. The Navy gave us the option of transferring to any of several colleges and universities. Gus decided to transfer to San Marcos, where his soon-to-be wife Maxine was enrolled. The following year, when our class of V-5ers received their orders to Pre-Flight, Gus requested discharge from the Navy, and he and Maxine stayed at San

Marcos and got their degrees in Education.

Gus and Maxine settled in Houston and raised five sons. During the next 45 years we saw little of each other. My wife Annie and I and our six children visited them on occasion, but it was not until Gus's limp proved to be bona fide and required hip surgery that we got together again for any length of time.

In 1993 the old courthouse in Hillsboro burned to the ground. Just about everyone who had lived in Hill County during the past hundred years, and was still alive, rallied to the cry to rebuild. Willie Nelson, who grew up in Abbot, six miles south on Waco Street, brought his band to the courthouse steps; and, just like in the movie, *Field of Dreams*, the people came. It was the largest reunion the town had ever seen. It lasted for several days. Gus was there in a wheelchair. His wife, Maxine, and my wife, Annie, and all the old gang enjoyed pushing Gus around town and up close to hear Willie.

But Gus did not get to see Willie when he came back to celebrate the completion of the restoration project. Gus died while the ruins of the courthouse were still on the ground. Annie and I were back in Florida when I received a call from a friend who told me that Gus was in bad shape. I called him at his home just two hours before he died. My intention was to persuade him to go back to the hospital and give the doctors another chance. But as we talked I realized that Gus had already fought a long tough battle and that he was tired. I listened as he told me a few details, and my mind could not help but remember better times.

I imagined him again, high in the air, smiling for the camera while catching the winning touchdown for Hillsboro High. I remembered his limp to Brown's Drug store on Saturday mornings and the sound of him chomping on an apple in our room at Southwestern.

It is rumored that shortly after Gus's death one of his sons made a quiet trip from Houston to Hillsboro. He came at night and sneaked through the barricades that surrounded the old courthouse. Then he spread his father's ashes throughout the charred remains of a very special patriarchal landmark in Texas.

Despite the years, I can sometimes feel again the shock of Gus's blow, when he did for me the biggest favor one man can do for another — the "coward cure." On the night that Gus died, his voice was not all that different from the moment years ago when he flashed a very special Hilton grin, held up his arms, and said, "Peace Old Buddy. Let's get some sleep."

Tommy Thomson grew up in Spanish-oriented southern California during the golden era of Hollywood. He was the son of a movie actor who starred in westerns in the days of Tom Mix, Hopalong Cassidy and Gene Autry. Tommy's dad never became a familiar household name. He died at an early age from blood poisoning, which resulted from an accident that occurred while filming a movie on location.

Tommy, although six feet, three-inches tall, with broad shoulders like his dad, did not follow in his father's footsteps. He chose instead to become a Navy pilot. He was one of the early Flying Midshipmen, nearly a year ahead of me in flight training. Our paths crossed when I reported aboard VA-195 at NAS Alameda in the fall of 1949.

The squadron was preparing to depart on a Pacific cruise, and Tommy and I flew a small twin-engine utility aircraft (the Navy's SNB) to Arizona to pick up needed aircraft parts for our squadron's AD Skyraiders.

Tommy was senior, insofar as seniority exits between ensigns, and had some experience flying the SNB. He was pilot in command. I had no experience in the SNB and flew as copilot.

The trip was routine to Arizona. We loaded the aircraft parts and headed back for California. It was well after dark by the time we got into the air and near midnight when we crossed the mountains east of San Jose near the southern end of San Francisco Bay.

The weather was terrible, with a heavy mix of thunderstorms and total darkness, shattered constantly by brilliant lightning. There was extreme turbulence that sometimes bounced the SNB hundreds of feet up or down in seconds. The lightning flashes were bothering us, so we turned on overhead white lights in the cockpit to cushion the effect. Destroying our night vision was of no concern, vision outside the aircraft was useless. Tommy needed only to see his instruments and I to see navigation charts and radio dials.

In those days radio navigation consisted of a device referred to by pilots as a "coffee grinder." It was a low-frequency radio receiver with a small hand crank to tune in various stations. In bad weather there was a lot of static; radio signals would come and go, dependent upon the mood of the equipment and the outside atmosphere. Reception was similar to today's AM radio as compared to FM, except that in the case of the old coffee grinder, reception was even worse in thunderstorms and lightning.

Navigation consisted of flying along airways — "Highways in the Sky," according to some airline public-relations types. They consisted of fixed-transmission beacons on the ground, which were about 30 miles apart. They transmitted a radio signal that could be picked up by the coffee-grinder receiver. The beacons transmitted a Morse code A (.–) and an N (–.). They were heard in the pilot's ear as dit-dah and dah-dit. When the aircraft was on course the two signals blended together and became a solid humming sound. If the pilot allowed his aircraft to drift left of course, he received a dit-dah; and if he drifted right of course, he received a dah-dit. In addition, each beacon had its own identification so that the pilot could be certain that he was steering toward his chosen destination.

About 30 miles west of San Jose, in the foothills of the mountains over which Tommy Thomson and I flew that night, there was then a beacon called, "La Jolla Intersection."

We were flying at 12,000 feet, to clear the mountain range with as much safety as we could. We were near the maximum altitude for the SNB, and the severe turbulence could bounce us 500 feet up or down very quickly.

Tommy had his hands full, trying to hold altitude and direction. As the beacon behind us began to fade into total static, Tommy asked me to tune in La Jolla Intersection.

I looked at the map and searched for "La-Hoy-Ya," which is the way we would spell such a name in Hillsboro, Texas. Hillsboro is a long way from Spanish-speaking Mexico, and further still from Southern California.

After searching frantically in the area of the chart that I knew we were in, I could not find a beacon with spelling that sounded anything like La-Hoy-Ya.

Finally, knowing that we were running out of time, that we were in the mountains at night with extreme turbulence and blinding lightning, and that we were without any type of navigational aid, Tommy grabbed the map from my hands and passed control of the aircraft to me.

Over the intercom he said, "Keep it straight and level." His tone of voice added: Surely there is something in this cockpit that you can do.

Tommy quickly found La Jolla beacon on the chart, cranked in the identification code and listened as the voiced-over signal said very clearly, "La Jolla Intersection." He then took control of the aircraft from me and flew back to the center of the beam.

When we were at last squared away and had made our turn from La Jolla to the airway that would lead us to Alameda, Tommy made a descent to a lower and smoother altitude. We were out of the lightning.

There had been silence in the cockpit for some time. I was reviewing in my mind my stupid mistake and searching for someway to redeem my lost pride.

Finally, Tommy pressed his intercom button and said,

"For a damn dumb Texan you fly straight and level pretty good. Do you think you could also turn off that white light, give us a preliminary landing check, and call approach control? It is spelled A-L-A-M-E-D-A."

Since that day I have become a man who is well versed in the peculiarities of the Spanish "J" and the Texas "H."

Chapter 7

What was once the L&N railroad station in Pensacola, Florida, is now the lobby of the Pensacola Grand Hotel. Old steam-powered trains from the 1940s and 1950s no longer pull alongside. Gone are those marvelous chugging, unsharpened sounds that blended so spectacularly with the hissing of escaping steam and the resonant clanging of high-pitched bells. Gone is the intense screeching of metal wheels pressing and crunching against steel rails. Vanished also is the sight and smell of warm misty clouds swirling from hot boilers. Too soon the little clouds rose. And too soon they disappeared. All that remains for those who ponder and reminisce about such matters are a few gentle keepsakes: memories of a time that is no more.

Today, businessmen and businesswomen intermingle with vacationers in the lobby of the Pensacola Grand. They circulate and converse in soft voices. Nearby, others dine on beautiful old china and sip from elegant crystal. All are surrounded with quiet, polite sounds. Some discreetly study the crowd.

Occasionally, a few men with gray hair or shiny tops

where ample lustrous strands once grew will enter the lobby. Anticipation and interest show on their faces. They study the room carefully and converse in voices that rise slightly above the steady hum of the crowd. Soon, one in the new group will point and grab a friend's shoulder. Another will give slaps on the back to his nearby buddies. Those observing can detect the beginnings of a debate among the group as to where, exactly, the old ticket counter stood.

The newcomers then move to a nearby bar and order drinks to be concocted from brands that were popular 50 years ago. After a drink or two, the new arrivals begin to talk with their hands. Soon their hands become symbols for two airplanes in a vicious dogfight, and those observing know that once again old Navy pilots have returned to their genesis. For a few moments these aging and now gentle souls will relive another time — a time when they were prepared and eager to begin one of the most exciting adventures of their lives.

Perhaps someday there will be a plaque over the aged depot door that is now a part of the Pensacola Grand. It should state with clear and simple words that through these portals passed many of the men who wrote the early history of Naval Aviation.

Beginning well before World War I, and continuing through the Korean War, they came, most of them through the doors of the old L&N depot. Today they still come, but usually by jet or automobile.

I first entered the depot in early October of 1947, remembering one of the Navy's many statements of wisdom: "If you cannot be good, make damn sure that you are lucky."

In early 1947 the Navy transferred preflight training from Otumwa, Iowa, to Pensacola, Florida. When class 20-47 (the twentieth preflight class of 1947) reported for duty, it was to sunny Florida rather than the ice and snow of Iowa.

Pensacola's climate is not that of Miami's, but it is on the Gulf of Mexico in what is geographically southern Alabama, but politically Florida. It is a town proud of its history and sugar-white beaches.

A little-known fact is that Pensacola was the first recorded settlement in the United States. Fourteen hundred men and women of stout heart sailed to Pensacola Beach from Spain in 1559 and were quickly blown into oblivion by a hurricane. It was a long six years before St. Augustine became our country's first permanent settlement.

1947 was a significant year to begin military flight training. Class 20-47 was sworn in as Flying Midshipmen on October 13. The next day a pilot named Chuck Yeager rolled a little dart-shaped jet into a dive over a desert in California. He flew himself into history. His was the first documentation that an aircraft could exceed the speed of sound and remain in one piece. The Jet Age had truly begun, and not long after (in May 1949) a young man named Neil Armstrong was sworn in as a Flying Midshipman at Pensacola Preflight. Later he would take mankind's first step on the moon. Times, they were a'changing!

But those of us in class 20-47 were not concerned with Chuck Yeager or man's first trip to the moon. We were not interested in much of anything that was not related to getting through the next day of training.

As soon as we were assigned a room and issued clothing, we reported to the gym for a physical. The test was simple: We stood in front of a bench, each of us with a bucket alongside, and began to step onto the bench and then back to the floor, over and over again until we commenced to throw up in the bucket. A marine sergeant stood alongside to record times. Just a few weeks before, I had been playing football in the heat of a Texas August/September on a Hillsboro Junior College team that went on to win the Texas championship that year. I thought I was in pretty good physical condition, but I was nowhere near the last one in our class to begin throwing up.

After the conditioning check we selected a sport in which we desired to compete while in Preflight. Thanks to Gus Hilton, I chose boxing. One of my preflight roommates was a fellow named Cal Wilson. Cal, who was from New Jersey, had 30 fights as a professional lightweight before joining the Navy. I was a light heavy, but boxing is boxing and the basics are the same. During the next couple of months Cal taught me a lot and I wound up fighting a fellow midshipman named Chuck Spann for the preflight championship.

Chuck was fresh from the University of South Carolina, where as a sophomore he had been runner-up national collegiate champion. We went three rounds. Both of us had a good left. The difference was that Chuck also had a very fast knockout right. So during my training for the fight, Cal wisely instructed me to concentrate on throwing my left and circling right. The strategy worked fine, but by the end of the first round I knew that Chuck was beating me on points because he was the aggressor. So toward the end of the second round, a little of Grandpa George-type thinking sneaked into my own thoughts and I made a stupid mistake. I decided to throw a few rights and try to win the fight. The first right I threw was countered by Chuck and within a split second his return right whistled past my head with such force that the breeze alone nearly knocked me down.

My mama "did not raise no dumb boy," so that was the last right I threw during the entire fight. When the bell rang to end the second round, Cal Wilson gave me hell.

"Atkinson," he said, "if you want to end this fight on your feet, you had best forget trying to be a hero. Just stay hidden behind that left and circle the wagons right."

I stayed on my feet for the third round and Chuck won the fight on points. I also made the decision then and there that I had better learn to fly airplanes real good, because my days as a professional fighter would be short.

Chuck went on to win about everything in boxing in the Navy. After flight training we went separate ways — Chuck to the East Coast and me to the West. I did not talk with him again for 50 years. When I did, he told me that he got out of the Navy early and went back to the University of South Carolina. He fulfilled his dream of winning the light-heavy collegiate national championship. This made me feel good and I told Chuck, "My twenty-two grandkids will be proud to know that their grandfather was in the ring with a real champion."

Chuck's reply was quick and spoken in his dry no-nonsense South Carolina accent, "Stop the bull, Atkinson. You were good."

While I was saying thank you, I was remembering the feel of Chuck's right as it grazed my check and whistled past my head. I was also thinking that Chuck was a wise and modest man to refrain from adding the words, "But I was a little better."

There was a lot more to preflight than boxing. We spent many hours in a classroom learning navigation and weather, how an aircraft engine works, and how the wings provide the lift to keep everything in the air. It was interesting and we all wanted to learn, but most of us were more interested in starting actual flight training.

On Saturday mornings several of us would go down to the hangers at Chevalier field, which was the original Pensacola Naval Air Station. It was within walking distance of our preflight barracks, and it was there that the Navy did major repair work on the hundreds of aircraft used in the Pensacola area. Test flights were often needed and it was easy to bum a ride in an empty seat.

It was on such a morning that I first met Hap Harris, a fellow midshipman who was a few classes ahead of me. Some of us were grabbing a quick lunch, when Hap began to describe his morning flight with a South American who had just won his Navy wings. The hop was in an SNJ, a two-seat, low-wing trainer that was due for a test flight following engine change. This normally meant a dull routine of flying circles in designated locations near an airfield. But Hap's pilot had other ideas. Thirty minutes after takeoff they were low over the farmlands of North Florida leaving dust trails. Hap swore that they had to climb to clear fences. But it was when they flew low over a wide river and under a railroad bridge that Hap became really disturbed.

The SNJ has a rear-view mirror in the front cockpit. It can be used in a manner similar to those in automobiles, but it can also be adjusted to see the face of the person sitting in back. After flying under the bridge, Hap looked up to see the South American's reflection grinning at him from the front cockpit, saw his lips moving, and heard a heavily accented voice in his earphones: "Was da mahder? You don' wan' to die?"

Hap graduated a short time later and left for flight training. I had no way of knowing then, but our paths would cross again.

A few weeks later class 20-47 completed preflight and we ran into a large winter pile-up of midshipmen waiting to start flight training. To make some use of slack time, the Navy sent us on a cruise to Cuba. For most of us it was our first time at sea, and when we checked aboard the USS Wright, we were excited to be going somewhere and doing something different, even if flying had to wait awhile.

The USS Wright was a small aircraft carrier from World War II. When in Pensacola, it was used for training purposes. Less than a year later many of us would make our first carrier landings on the Wright's old wooden deck on which we then walked, played touch football, and sometimes on a hot night brought a blanket and pillow from our bunkroom and slept.

The USS Wright was my first experience with Navy shipboard life. The lessons I learned on that short trip stayed with me for many years to follow. First, I learned that midshipmen aboard the Wright were men without a country. Officers were officers and had their own space. The same with the enlisted men below the rating of chief. The chiefs had their space also. Nowhere — aboard ship or on shore, except in the large bunkroom where we slept — was there a designated place for midshipmen to relax. We were not officers and we were not enlisted men.

Finally, after our first liberty in Cuba, the chiefs decided to adopt us. We were invited to their club, and for the next several weeks we received a lot of special training. In effect, we were taught with subtle communication that the chiefs run the United States Navy. Additional information was instilled so that in the years ahead we would never become confused with fuzzy thoughts to the contrary. Years later, when I was Flight Deck Officer aboard the USS Essex, my old "chief's training" proved to be extremely valuable.

When we returned from Cuba, we reported to NAS Whiting, a training field 30 miles from Pensacola, near Milton, Florida. At long last we were ready to begin flight training.

The Navy's SNJ was one of the great training aircraft of its day. In this bright yellow, low-wing "Texan," which the Air Force in their strange lingo call the "T6," I began my training to become a Navy pilot. Although I had over 50 hours of flying in light aircraft and had earned my private license in civilian aviation, flying the SNJ was the same as starting all over. Navy instructors are not interested in their students' past flying experience; their job is to teach you the Navy way. So, for that first flight in the

SNJ, I cleared my mind of the past and concentrated on making it the same as my first airplane ride when I was six years old.

I can still remember the feel of leaving the ground and starting to climb. Despite engine noise, everything becomes quiet. And despite speed, everything slows down. Large things become small and the pressing problems that confront us while earthbound are somehow set aside. We become conscious that we are on top of everything and that we can see everything as it happens. Some of those who stay at it for a long time are sometimes engulfed with the odd sensation that they can see even that which has not yet happened. Perhaps that is why some pilots tend to drink a little and talk a lot, particularly with other pilots.

Today, when flying as a passenger on a large jet, I am quick to note that all of the above is not necessarily true. But then I close my eyes and remember the feel of a small propeller-driven aircraft, as the wheels softly break loose from the silky feel of a freshly harvested hay field. I remember that marvelous bouquet of sensations that take control when the smell of early morning country fills my lungs. A feeling of total relaxation envelops my mind and body. That old perception of slowing down, of leaving all worldly cares behind, of being on top of everything, returns with all the impact of those early morning flights with Dumas in the old Taylorcraft.

Such words are not meant to be spoken, however. They serve best when carefully stored with our most secret thoughts — reflections from the past, like the phrase from a great old song: "Gentle on my mind."

My first flight instructor in the Navy was a small red-faced man named Cheney. During the early flights he did most of the flying, instructing me precisely on how to handle the SNJ while performing various maneuvers. I remember that everything felt bigger and stronger and heavier than the small Piper Cubs I had flown. The wheels retracted by moving a large metal lever, and the engine was louder and much more powerful. But after a few flights the SNJ began to feel more and more like the Cubs that I had flown from a hayfield in Hillsboro, Texas.

Then the day came when I made several good landings. After the last one, Cheney left the engine running, hopped out, and watched as I made my first solo flight in a Navy aircraft. I remember seeing myself in a reflection against the glass canopy. My helmet and goggles looked like a picture on a recruiting poster. My flight suit was partially covered with a yellow life jacket and I was thinking, "Here I am!" I even turned to look and make sure that no one was in the back seat. I was a Navy pilot, flying all by myself. I hoped that my brother-cousin, Billy, could see me.

Then began many months of flying solo with occasional check rides by Cheney and other instructors who graded progress, followed by formation flying, instrument flying, night flying, aerobatics, and gunnery. Finally, came carrier-landing practice to learn to land an aircraft aboard a carrier.

"Clang! Clang! Clang! General Quarters! General

Quarters! All hands man your battle stations. This is no drill!"

A shattering, nerve-racking sound familiar to many Navy men woke us a little after daybreak. Red and Gootch and Jason, my other roommates, were snoring and stirring, trying to wake.

I stumbled to the phone and called our squadron's ready-room to see what the hell was going on. Nick Redeye, an Indian chief and World War II pilot recalled for Korea, had the duty and answered the phone.

"For god's sake, Tex, get some help down here! This smoke is going to kill me. I'm on the deck under the desk and there is only a few feet of air left."

Later, Nick would tell me that when the phone rang he had been searching for it with his hands from beneath the desk, trying to keep his head below the level of deadly smoke. Nick said that panic was setting in and that the ring of the phone was like a sound from heaven.

I dashed to the flight deck and found a rescue group and told them where to find Lt. Redeye. Somehow, even in all the confusion, they got Nick out in time.

What had happened was that a flight of AD night fighters had landed at dawn. To clear the deck for the next launch, they were dropped on the deck-edge elevator to the hanger deck. As one of the ADs was being pushed off the elevator, a 20-millimeter wing cannon fired accidentally. The shell hit an empty wing tank attached to a jet's folded wing. The jet was parked forward on the hanger deck with nearly empty wing tanks that were filled with volatile gas fumes.

The wing tank exploded and set off a chain reaction

that caused all hell to break loose. The hanger deck was jammed with aircraft — many of the planes were loaded with armament. The fire spread quickly out of control and intense heat began to set off bombs, gas tanks, rockets — anything that would explode or burn.

Jim Shropshire, our flight surgeon, was up and working in his office over the hanger deck. When the explosions began, he ran onto the overhead walkway just in time to catch a load of shrapnel in his chest.

There was no one around to help with Jim's massive wounds, no one to offer compassion, no one to whom Jim could mutter a simple goodbye. Such a happening was ironic, because Jim was the guy who worked all night, trying to save Gene Moller, our Corsair pilot who crashed while in a night-carrier pattern at Santa Rosa.

Gene had lost his engine downwind on a pitch-black night at low altitude. His wheels and flaps were down. The Corsair hit the ground quickly, flipped onto its back and slid backwards in the muddy field. The massive crane used for such occasions bogged to its axles before going a hundred yards; gas fumes precluded any thought of using cutting torches; and despite the frantic efforts of everyone present, there was simply no way to budge the heavy fighter.

Gene was jammed in the cockpit. His windshield had served as a scoop while the Corsair slid inverted tail first. The mud jammed his body nearly double. Although not fatally injured, he could not take a deep breath. While others stood silently and held flashlights, Jim Shropshire dug and twisted himself beneath the inverted Corsair and held his fingers to Gene Moller's wrist for four hours.

After midnight most activity had ended. There was little sound in the darkness of the large desolate field except the murmur of Jim Shropshire's voice, softly giving encouragement to a young man slowing dying of asphyxiation.

Then, after all those hours, the comforting whispers stopped. Jim squirmed himself back and out of the mud and slowly pulled himself to his feet. His back and arms were terribly cramped. There were tears soaked into his cheeks, which we could not see but knew were there.

Jim said very simply, "He is gone."

And after all that, in the confusion following the explosion on the Boxer, no one knew about Jim Shropshire until later, when his body was found. The explosion that got Jim, killed everyone in the overhead medical office.

When I ran from our room to the flight deck, I did not take time to dress. I was in my navy-issue white boxer shorts. My pants were half on, and I had slipped my feet into a pair of unlaced flight deck shoes. I made my way across the part of the hanger deck where there had been a gruesome explosion but no fire.

I realized I was walking in something slippery and that I was about to lose my shoes. Then I saw it was blood and saw the half torso and all the other bodies. Most of them were under damaged aircraft. Finally, I made my way to an outside ladder and climbed to the flight deck.

Later, when I got to thinking about everything, I realized that those bloody and battered pieces were the only dead bodies that I could remember seeing clearly during all of the Korean War.

War from the air is so very neat — just downright squeaky clean.

Chapter 8

On weekends, when we were not learning how to fly the SNJ, we often went into Pensacola or out to the beach to unwind. We also had a Midshipmen's Club on the air station that was called ACRAC, a carryover from the days when it was known as the Aviation Cadets Recreation and Amusement Center. On Friday nights there was always a big dance at ACRAC, and girls from town would come out to meet anxious young men who hungered to be Navy pilots.

I met and dated a couple of local girls for a few weeks, and then one of them introduced me to her cousin, Annie Sanchez. Unlike Janice's introducing me to her cousin, Suzie, this introduction was for the purpose of moving me on. And that it did.

Within a few weeks Annie and I were dating steady. She was the oldest of Phil and Sabra Sanchez's seven daughters and one son. Her family dated back very close to the time that Pensacola's first settlers were blown away by a hurricane, and Annie's home was always filled with aunts and uncles and cousins. Everybody talked at the same time and the sound was like heaven. I had always longed to be part of a large family, and suddenly I felt as though I had found a home. Her one brother and six sisters were scattered in age, all the way down to three or four years old.

I liked going to the big old house that had been moved back from the water so that her father could build his apartment houses. For the past 40 years, Phil had been everything at the San Carlos Hotel, from shine boy to assistant manager. The San Carlos was built in the center of downtown Pensacola shortly after the turn of the century, close to the time that the Wright brothers made their first flight. From those early 1900s until the end of the Vietnam War, the San Carlos was a part of Naval Aviation history. Most of the men and women who helped make that history, at one time or another, had either been a guest of the San Carlos, drank at its bar, or danced on the floor of its huge ballroom. Thus Phil Sanchez came to know many of the early Navy flyers, men whose bronze likenesses now line the passageways at the Naval Aviation Museum. Some he knew from the time they were cadets or ensigns fresh out of Annapolis, until they were Admirals. Some of the same young men that Phil's house detectives booted out of his hotel for sneaking young girls into their rooms were later national heroes with their pictures on every newspaper in the country. The story I remember best is of Pappy Boyington, who later led the famous Black Sheep Squadron of World War II fame, won the Congressional Medal, and survived the hell of a Japanese prisoner of war camp. Pappy was caught trying to sneak one of Phil's younger sisters, Annie's Aunt Charlotte, into the bar after Phil had forbidden all his sisters from coming near the San Carlos.

Shortly after I met Annie, I decided that I had to have another automobile. I had not owned one since I sold the Model-A to take flying lessons, and now the time had come. My running mate at the time was a fellow named Bob Finley. We called Bob "Gator Bait" because he was small and from Louisiana, and because he insisted that when he was just a kid his father had tied a rope around his neck and drug him through the bayous of the back country in the hopes of catching a gator.

Bob was smart. After Navy duty he made millions as an architect and heavy construction builder in Louisiana. At the time Annie and I started dating, Bob had just met a new girlfriend and decided that owning an automobile might not be a bad idea. So one Saturday we went to a car lot in Pensacola, and after the salesman stated a price of $175 for an old 1935 Chevrolet, I asked if he would take $150.

The Chevy was a total wreck. Although a sedan, it had only two doors that opened from the front and one of them was tied on with bailing wire. All of the windows were broken, and the bottom of the car was badly rusted. In later years I would have passed it by even to strip and make a beach buggy, but at the time all I could see was what the car would look like after Bob and I finished our rebuilding at the Navy's hobby shop.

As soon as I asked the salesman if he would take $150 for the Chevy, Bob Finley kicked me hard on the leg. If the salesman noticed, he gave no indication, he just smoothly stated that he would have to check with his manager. He was back in two minutes, smiling and congratulating me on driving a hard bargain, but, yes, "For Navy, they would let the car go for $150."

Somehow Bob and I managed to drive the car under its own power to the base, and with an escort by security got it as far as the hobby shop. For the next several weeks I was busy. Bob worked with me for a while and then one day he said, "Tex, I am going to make you a real deal. I am going to bow out and give you my half of the Chevy."

I was both happy and sad. It hurt me to know that Bob Finley thought so little of my expertise in picking automobiles that he would just give away his half. At the same time I was pleased to know that I now owned a car all by myself and could do with it as I pleased.

Within a month I had rebuilt all the rusted-out brake connections, installed Plexiglas for windows, and replaced the bailing wire that held one door on with neat looking rope. Annie made seat covers out of worn curtains and pretty soon the old Chevy was looking half respectable. I still had to use a stick propped against the dashboard to hold the transmission in third gear, and the engine continued to burn a lot of oil, but there was not enough time between flying and classroom study to do much more.

Somehow I managed to get the Chevy past the base inspectors and got a sticker to drive on and off the air station. After Annie and I had double-dated with Finley and his new girlfriend, and with several other classmates and their dates, the aged Chevy began to acquire a reputation for dubious reliability. At first everyone was reluctant to get in the thing; but after many good liberties, when our antiquated auto got us there and got us back, with no more than a push or two, Annie and I decided that the name "Old Chevy" was not really descriptive of our automobile. We concluded that a much more dignified moniker was needed. We then changed the name of our gorgeous pile of black junk to "P.M.," our abbreviation for "Perpetual Motion."

Several weeks after we had P.M. running pretty good, Christmas holidays came around. I decided to drive to Texas. I had not been home for a long while and Christmas was the time to be there. So that I could make good use of all the days off, I checked off the base at midnight. It was a chilly December night and I was suited out neatly in my dress blue uniform. I put my bags in the back seat of P.M. and headed for Hillsboro.

A few hours later I was going up a long hill in Mississippi. It was one of those pitch-black nights with no moon, and suddenly the headlights on the dilapidated Chevy went totally black. There were lights coming over the hill ahead and bright glares from another car coming up behind. This was well before the days of interstates and four lanes and wide areas alongside to pull off. All I could think to do as I spun the wheel hard right was to get off the road.

I felt P.M. bump its way down a steep embankment and then the sudden stop as the battered Chevy half buried itself in a drainage ditch alongside the highway. If the other cars' drivers saw me as they whistled past, they gave no indication.

There was nothing then but silence and the night sounds of whatever animals and squirmy things are awake at three o'clock in the morning in the wilds of central Mississippi.

I managed to get the one good door of the Chevy open and crawled up the embankment to the side of the highway. I brushed off my blues as best I could and tried to look dignified. I did not want to be confused with your run-of-the-mill hitchhiker and gave little thought to the fact that the few squirmy night things in central Mississippi that were still awake couldn't care less.

Occasionally a car or truck would speed by, but their drivers paid no attention. Then, after a particularly long period of time during which there had been no highway sounds at all, I heard a rumble of noise and the far-off harmony of singing voices coming from over the hill that I had been climbing before taking to the ditch.

Soon, a huge truck with a flatbed in back pulled alongside and stopped. There were two guys in the cab and four on the flatbed and they had all been singing at the top of their voices, until they saw me at the side of the road. The old Chevy was totally out of sight in the ditch, and with my dark uniform I was probably hard to see.

The singing stopped and the driver of the truck, who had a deep southern voice said, "Well, what do we have here? Fellows, I think we have done found us one of them Navy types and he is all dressed up in his pretty sailor suit."

Then the driver opened his door, took a long drag from his bottle of beer, looked straight at me and asked, "What's the trouble Navy Boy?"

I told my story as quickly as I could.

Within a few minutes everyone on the truck had crawled down into the ditch and examined P. M. They discussed the situation among themselves, then the driver and the others got onto the truck and turned it around on the highway so that it was headed back up the hill. Before they left, the men on the flatbed handed me a paper sack with several bottles of cold beer inside. They told me to just relax and assured me that they would be back. It seemed like forever before I again heard loud singing. By then I had downed a few beers myself and was amazed at the improvement in the group's harmony. I found myself humming along to sounds that were definitely better than total silence interrupted only by chirping and squealing night sounds.

The beer-drinking Mississippi loggers had gone back to the mill where they worked and commandeered a much larger truck, with a crane mounted on the flatbed. Within half an hour they had crawled in and under P.M., through the water and mud in the drainage ditch, and snuggled a sling completely around the half-buried automobile. When they started the motor on the huge crane, the battered Chevy was literally jerked from the drainage ditch and sat neatly on the road.

I got in, and Perpetual Motion started like it was 1935 all over again and some salesman was proudly showing her off on the showroom floor.

I tried to give the crew some of the few dollars I had, but they would not take a penny. One of them said, "We're proud to do it sailor boy. If them Japs and Germans ever give us any more trouble, then you can make it even with us."

So in the early morning light of a chilly December day, from the deep backcountry of central Mississippi, I was again on my way to Hillsboro, Texas.

Strange, how some names get away. Some don't. I remember that one AD nearly made it to the beach, about 50 miles north of San Francisco and the other, number 513, went straight in from 8,000 feet. The date was Friday, the 13th of October 1949.

Don Van Slooten and I had received our ensign's bars early that morning. The skipper of our squadron, Harry White, had presided over a quick and informal ceremony in his office before the first flight of the day.

During the five years between the end of World War II in 1945 and the beginning of the Korean War in 1950, the Navy's Aviation Cadet program was on hold. It was replaced during those years by the Navy's Flying Midshipmen program. An admiral named Holloway somehow found dollars for flight training, even though the Navy had few dollars to spend. The new program turned out Navy and Marine pilots as fast as Harry Truman's administration could squeeze dollars from congress — not very fast. History, as usual, was repeating itself.

As soon as World War II ended, politicians became extremely sensitive to the American voter's proclamation: "Peace time! War's over! We need butter, not bombs!"

Consequently, tax dollars went many places, but very few were tagged for the military. After two years of college, we were sworn in as Flying Midshipmen and ordered to flight training. Those who were still around after two years were commissioned as ensigns. We won our wings when we graduated from advanced training and were assigned to a fleet squadron.

We were then fully qualified for carrier duty, flying combat-ready aircraft, but without ensign bars. Hence the name, "Flying Midshipmen." Several of our group flew in combat, and some were killed while still midshipmen. They were earning $112.50 monthly. A few self-appointed wits — those with no class — have said that we were "cheap warriors."

Thus, Friday the 13th of October 1949 was Van's and my day to become officers and gentlemen. With this extraordinary accomplishment came the option to move a notch up the social ladder. Some of our group were known to celebrate by switching from beer and salty dogs to brandy Alexanders and scotch. The same opportunity was afforded the remaining survivors of the 20th Pensacola preflight class of 1947, wherever they happened to be.

Immediately following the ceremony, I suited out to fly wing on the Skipper in a division of four ADs. This was "the old man's" standard procedure for checking the flying skills of newcomers to his squadron. Van Slooten was scheduled for another time.

Harry White was my first fleet squadron Skipper. I could have done a lot worse. He was a quiet guy, near bashful sometimes, but he could fly. He had been awarded the Navy Cross and other medals for action in World War II. He wore just three, under the lapel of his blues. They were positioned so that you never saw the blue and white of the Cross. We ensigns thought this was the coolest.

That Friday morning Harry led our division west from Alameda, then out to sea, well north of the Bay Area. Our first drill for the day was to practice rendezvousing. We climbed to 8,000 feet, moved into right echelon, and the skipper broke left. In a few seconds I followed, then number three, then number four. When we were all in a straight line, Harry began a wide left turn. The rest of us turned inside to catch up and reform our division.

I joined alongside the skipper in pretty good shape, careful not to throw up a wing and block him from sight — a maneuver not recommended for check rides. About the time I was comfortably in position, I slid my AD under Harry to his right wing. It was then that I heard the single radio transmission.

"Mayday!"

It was not a voice in cold panic, like some I would hear later, just quick and urgent. Harry immediately turned hard left. All I could do was add power, stay tight on his wing, and hold on.

I could see enough to know that the Skipper was trying to spot numbers three and four. After a short time he told me to orbit the area and to call rescue, give them our location and tell them that we had an emergency in the area. Harry then broke off and headed for the beach. It was after landing and listening to the debrief that I was able to learn what happened.

Numbers three and four had collided just behind us. Number four went straight in, probably minus a wing; and number three, without power or communications, started a long controlled glide straight for the nearest land. The skipper tracked the path of number three by flying east until he intersected the coastline north of San Francisco. A few miles short of land he found a tire, an oil slick, and a little floating debris from number three's AD.

Harry seemed convinced that number three had been trapped in the cockpit due to damaged canopy railings caused by the collision. Later, he wrote to the Navy's Bureau of Aeronautics asking that some sort of quick disconnect for the AD canopy be installed.

I never heard mention of the subject again. During the years from 1950 to the end of the Vietnam War, ADs flew thousands of missions — all with the same canopy design we used that Friday the 13th in 1949.

Harry was successful, however, in deleting the number 513 from VA-195 squadron aircraft. To my knowledge it was never used again — but for me the number 13 remained a problem.

Raised by an Irish mother, I grew up deathly afraid of black cats, ladders, spilled salt, and a multitude of other superstitions. After the mid-air on the 13th, the thought occurred to me that Van Slooten or I might have been the 13th ensign commissioned that day. There was no simple way of knowing. Our class was scattered all over — some in the Mediterranean, some in the Pacific, some in three other stateside time zones, and Van and I in California.

Then our Air Group went aboard the USS Boxer for a long operational tour in the Pacific, and I got lucky. I gave a fortuneteller in Singapore a few dollars and she delivered to me one of the great purchases of my life.

She revealed to me ancient and seldom disclosed

knowledge, a secret human movement, a gesture, passed carefully from one select eastern culture to another, century after century, beginning with the earliest of mankind and his fear of emerging into daylight from the darkness of a cave. At least that is what the old nomad told me; and in Hillsboro, Texas, we were taught to listen to our elders.

The old gypsy's revelation has abolished superstition from my mind. In addition, this gesture to the gods, this simple movement of muscle and concentration of mind, has given me a protective shield from danger that has lasted a lifetime. Being the compassionate and magnanimous person that I am, I pass it on for the betterment of those wise enough to recognize a class act when they find one:

Take the index and middle fingers of the right hand and press them three times against the right thumb. Speed does not matter. Just press three times and think clearly about what you want to accomplish. If a black cat selects that precise moment to cross your path, surely such a rare happening, plus the finger and thumb action, can do nothing but bring good fortune.

Regardless of what premonition has entered your mind, this procedure is guaranteed to immediately remove anxiety caused by superstition. Premonitions of doom that engulf your mind are immediately replaced with the sweet calming assurance that an impending bonanza of good happenings are headed your way. (Jackie Gleason's enchanting and melodious, "How Sweet It Is!" contained a sly ring of truth that left no doubt in my mind that the old boy had been to Singapore.)

The thumb-finger mystique has worked for me through two tours in Korea, when at least once I was positive that I was being launched on a one-way flight. It worked raising six children. It remains in use today with 20-plus grandchildren.

Truth, however, is sometimes not quickly accepted by all. My wife, whom I know best after nearly 50 years of intimate partnership, is still reluctant to admit that she embraces her husband's suggestions. Nevertheless, on occasion, after a bit of sly marital observation, and by simply adding two and two, I have reason to speculate that even here, the old gypsy has worked her magic.

Also, while on that long peacetime cruise before Korea, at a bar somewhere in the Pacific, Harry White told a few of us how he won the Navy Cross. One of the more analytical in the group had made inquiries from various sources.

Our young researcher learned that Harry won the Cross for putting one of the first torpedoes, if not the first, into the Japanese battleship, Yamato. Those of you familiar with the sinking of the Yamato know that an enormous amount of ordnance struck the largest of the Japanese battleships before the old monster finally went down.

Over the years I have come to the conclusion that just about every Navy pilot who was in the area at the time, after a few drinks, "put a fish into the Yamato." Navy documents record the fact that Harry White really did.

After we brought up the subject, Harry explained to us that Japanese battleship gunners knew the speed, to the exact knot, of a TBM during a torpedo run. Since George

H. Bush's term as president, I am assuming that each of our citizens now knows what a TBM looks like and that it was the Navy's premier torpedo plane during World War II.

During a torpedo run, the most dangerous of Navy carrier operations, standard TBM procedure called for very low flight, just above the water, and with full throttle. During the run, the TBM and its crew were sitting ducks for every Japanese gun on every ship in the area.

Fresh in Harry White's mind while attacking the Yamato was the Battle of Midway, an extraordinary and deadly encounter between aircraft carriers. Midway was our first major victory in the Pacific in World War II, but it was not without cost. Torpedo Eight lost all its aircraft. Only one pilot survived, and another squadron suffered an almost identical fate.

Thus, when Harry White made his torpedo run against the Yamato, he stated that he was in such a state of panic — near hyperventilation — that he forgot to add full throttle. He made the entire run a few knots below top speed. Throughout the run all he saw was the bright flash of bursting shells just in front of his windshield. When he returned to his carrier, all the paint was burned from the leading edges of the wings and the nose of his TBM.

I have always suspected that Harry White knew well the old Singapore gypsy who became my lifetime friend. I have no doubt whatsoever that Harry was blessed with her protective shield long before I got there.

As for Don Van Slooten, when I started this story concerning a Friday the 13th in 1949, I had not heard from him since Korea. His life went one way and mine another; we lost touch.

Van and I had been together all through preflight and were roommates for two cruises with VA-195. He whipped all of us at tennis, from Pensacola to Singapore to Tokyo. He turned down an offer to leave the Navy and accept a college basketball scholarship when he was spotted playing in some intra-mural league in the Bay Area. He was a strict non-drinking Mormon from Utah, so when he drank a toast on his knees at the squadron reception when I married Annie, he used pure ginger ale.

I remember his crying profusely at the debrief, while describing how Hap Harris died in the cold waters off North Korea in early 1951. A bad day in January. Then, while doing research to write a story about Hap, who had been a good friend of both Van and myself, I discovered that Van was the only known witness to Hap's final moments. The skipper, Swede Carlson, and his wingman were not in a position to observe.

Thus began the search to find Don Van Slooten. Computer telephone name and number software is a great tool. Thanks to the help of another old preflight buddy who has such software and knows how to use it, the Don Van Slooten for whom we searched was found.

Don is very much alive and is settled with his large family in Salt Lake City. I understand he is still actively involved in the operation of Mormon hospitals and rest homes.

So this pretty well winds up the whereabouts of the players in my little tale, which began on a Friday the 13th in 1949. Except for the pilots of Number Three and Number Four, the ADs that collided in mid-air on that day.

The old Singapore gypsy taught me a lot, but as to the final destiny of these two men, even that wise old sage had no knowledge, only conjecture.

I wish I had met her earlier. Somehow I would have found a way to introduce the three of them. In the grand scheme of things it just might have made a difference.

Number Three and Number Four only needed a few more feet of space.

And for the lack thereof, they missed so very much.

Chapter 9

After Christmas I drove P.M. back to Pensacola, this time without the need for help from "good-ol' Mississippi boys." I spent New Year's with Annie. Primary training in the SNJ would soon be ending and our class would head for Corpus Christi, Texas, to begin advanced training. The last few days of Christmas holidays would be our last unhurried days for a long while.

Completing SNJ training entailed making 10 successful landings aboard a carrier. The USS Wright, our old Cuba cruise ship, was again operating out of Pensacola and class 20-47 was busy with what the Navy calls field carrier landing practice, or FCLP.

"What is it like to land aboard a carrier?" Navy pilots hear the question often, and most of us have created our own quick answers. "Just takes a little skill, guts, and daring!" is a pretty good answer when you are in a cocky mood. But the truth is that like many other things in life, landing an aircraft aboard a carrier is simply a learned procedure.

In the days of propellers and straight decks, the technique was to slow the aircraft down, drop the wheels and flaps, get the aircraft into a tail-low landing attitude, and then hang it on the propeller. This meant that you were just above stall speed but still flying level and holding altitude, so that when you cut power, the aircraft would drop quickly and the tailhook would catch a strong cable that stretched across the flight deck. The two main wheels would hit the deck about the same time that the wings totally stalled.

In those days your eyes were glued to the landing signal officer, called the LSO, who used colored paddles held in his hands to let you know if you were too high or too low or too fast or too slow. The goal of the pilot was to receive a "roger" signal from the LSO and maintain it throughout his carrier approach. This signaled "Perfect Pass - Keep It Coming!" To send this signal the LSO extended both arms sideways as far as he could and held them there. He looked similar to a theatrical preacher extending benediction to his congregation.

The final landing approach was made while still in a turn, so that the nose of the aircraft did not block the pilot's view of the LSO. Becoming proficient required practice, and most of this was done on a regular landing field. We flew the SNJ low, about a hundred feet above the ground down one side of the runway and then began a turn, always left, to land. The LSO stood alongside the end of the runway so that as you approached the runway he was on your left and you could see his signals clearly.

When the LSO felt that you were in good position to make a safe landing, he gave you the "cut," by bringing one paddle fast across his chest. At that instant you quickly chopped your power, then you held the attitude of the airplane, maybe a quick dip of the nose down and back if needed to drop a few feet, then the next moment you were on the runway, or when at sea, the flight deck.

If the LSO was not pleased with your approach, he gave you a "wave off," which was just like it sounds — he held the paddles high above his head and waved them back and forth. In the days of straight decks, the LSO was the final word. There was no second-guessing him. Once you cut the throttle, you were committed to land. If the tailhook missed all the cables, or "wires" as we called them, the aircraft was stopped by a large barrier to keep it from going into the pack of aircraft parked forward.

The barricade was made of nylon straps or cable stretched high above the flight deck. They were designed to stop the aircraft with as little damage as possible to the plane or to the pilot. An engine and propeller change for the aircraft and a brandy for the pilot were usually all that was needed to put things right again.

On January 12, 1949, flying the SNJ, I made 10 carrier landings on the USS Wright. During the first landing approach I was concentrating so hard on doing it right that I could have been on the shore flying an FCLP. I did not notice any real difference, until I realized that as I approached the LSO, everything seemed to be moving a little slower than on land. This was because the carrier was moving through the water at fast speed, and this in turn gave the sensation of flying slower. Then I felt the tailhook catch a wire and I was thrown hard against the shoulder straps.

Next, before I had time to think, my attention was directed to aircraft handlers on the flight deck. They were giving me signals so that I could taxi into position to take off and make another landing.

When the SNJ left the deck and I was airborne again, it hit me: I was a carrier pilot! I could not have seen my reflection in the canopy even if I had looked, because it was locked open; but I remember vividly the sudden flush of happiness that enveloped me, when I realized that I had actually landed an aircraft aboard a carrier. It gave me a surge of self-confidence that was very similar to what I felt when I saw Gus Hilton sprawled across Dave Medley's bed after I threw that first angry "right" in our room at Southwestern.

I trimmed the SNJ to fly as near hands-off as I could and turned downwind to start a new landing pattern. I looked at the sky above and the Gulf of Mexico below. The Gulf was glistening in the morning sun, reflecting just the hint of a distinctive shade of green that it some-times takes on, and the blue sky was carefully patterned with little puffs of floating white cumulus clouds. They moved smoothly above me.

I put the USS Wright on my left wing and checked my speed and altitude. Then a new feeling settled into my being. It was a feeling that would be a part of me for a long time to come. I realized that this was what I wanted to do for the rest of my life. I felt like pushing the mike button and telling anyone who was listening exactly how I felt. But even though I was inflicted with a slight case of euphoria, I had not lost my mind. Instead of pressing the mike, I just took deep breaths, indulged myself with new-found exhilaration, and concentrated on what I was doing.

In looking back, speaking my thoughts at that particular time might not have gotten me into too much trouble. The air-boss, who was in charge of all carrier flight operations, sitting high on the island of the carrier so he could see everything, and the LSO waiting on the fantail to wave me aboard again, and the Captain of the ship, listening on the bridge while guiding the ship, had probably felt what I felt when they were younger. It might have been good to bring back memories for them. But the unwritten rule of pilots is that you keep such thoughts to yourself, and never tie up the airways except when absolutely necessary.

The next nine landings were made while I held firmly to my new sensation, and while I was still basking in the glow of satisfaction from my first carrier landing.

The next day we flew our SNJs back to Pensacola, and that night Annie and I and a group from the twentieth class of 1947 celebrated. I had given Annie an engagement ring several weeks before, and we talked about Corpus and calculated how long it would be before I got my commission.

Then, within a week, I had all my gear packed in the Chevy and was on my way to Corpus Christi, Texas, to learn to fly the F4U Corsair.

It is sad to record, but Perpetual Motion never made it to Corpus. She had been using more and more oil, so much so that I stopped often at Billups Fill Up stations where they would give me used motor oil to fill a five-gallon can that I carried in back. By the time I got past Houston, P.M. was leaving a long stream of smoke behind. The compression in her engine was about gone, due to worn cylinder rings, and her power was slowly ebbing away. Between Houston and Galveston there is a towering bridge. In 1949 it was only two lanes, and by the time I made it to the top, which was very high above water, a long line of cars behind me were honking and drivers in a hurry were getting quite upset.

Then I started down the other side. The Chevy's brakes were gone, and by the time I made it to the bottom of the bridge I was holding on for dear life. I was going way too fast; the front wheels were shimmying, and all I could do was hope that I could find a clear place to head for if something pulled in front of me.

That night the weather turned bitter cold and the worn and weary heater was blowing out freezing air. By the time I made it to my Aunt Lois's and Uncle John's house in Texas City, I was bundled in about every piece of clothing I could find in my bag. When I parked what was left of Perpetual Motion in my aunt's front yard, it stayed. The next morning I caught the Greyhound to Corpus, and the next month my Aunt Lois paid someone to haul "that piece of junk" out of her yard.

My Aunt Lois is now approaching her nineties. My Uncle John has been gone for many years and my aunt lives in a nursing home in the Northwest near her son and daughter. I am able to visit with her when Annie and I go to Seattle to be with our son, Greg, and his family.

My Aunt Lois's mind is still sharp, and she remembers very clearly that cold day in January of 1949, when I left the old Chevy in the front of Uncle John Geer's and her home in Texas City. It was only three years after a ship carrying fertilizer had exploded in the harbor near their home and killed over 500 people. One of them came close to being my Uncle John, but he escaped with nothing more than a back full of shattered glass; yet he worked for three days and two nights helping find the injured and remove the dead from the rubble that was left along the waterfront.

She remembers most clearly having to pay someone $10 to have Annie's and my pride and joy — our beautiful P.M. — hauled to her final resting-place. And my Aunt Lois can still describe with detail "that pile of junk that looked terrible in my front yard."

But regarding whether I ever repaid her the $10 she was out, she cannot remember a thing.

Carlson's Canyon is now duly recorded as part of the history of Naval air operations in Korea. However, cold historical fact sometimes goes down a little better with a footnote or two. Swede Carlson was Commanding Officer of VA-195 during early 1951, when the squadron made many air strikes to knock out bridges in one strategic canyon in North Korea. So many strikes were made that the activity caught the attention of James Michener, who wrote a book that became a movie titled, *The Bridges at Toko Ri.*

Swede Carlson reported aboard as skipper of VA-195 shortly after the start of the Korean War. Soon thereafter, 195 was at NAS El Centro, in very southern California, for bombing and other practice, getting ready to go overseas.

Many of us in the squadron had just returned from a lengthy Western Pacific deployment that ended shortly before the war started. Our Executive Officer during the previous cruise was Dave Davidson, much respected by us junior officers as a pilot, a leader, and even as a father image.

Seldom does a day go by that something doesn't remind me of Dave's teachings:

"You must learn to separate the important from the unimportant."

"Don't practice parachute jumps."

"If it ain't broke, don't fix it."

"If you need to land and you are over a landing field, land!"

And most important, "When you work, WORK! When you play, PLAY!"

Dave Davidson would remain our XO for the first Korean tour with Swede Carlson.

At El Centro we flew from daylight until mid-morning. Due to extreme desert heat, we then shut down operations until near dark. The night shift would fly until 10 or 11P.M., then quit in time to partake of the nearby cultural center, Westmoreland, California.

No doubt, due to the war and rampant patriotism, Westmoreland was very much involved in the moral and physical well being of our fighting troops. Absolutely every museum and library in Westmoreland remained open until the last Navy pilot was fully refreshed with mental knowledge and instilled with enthusiasm to continue our quest to better the lot of all mankind.

Several of us junior officers, during thoughtful conversation over refreshments in one of the better libraries, and after due consideration of ample research material, came to the unanimous conclusion that our new skipper, Swede Carlson, was "up-tight."

Although friendly, and very competent as an aviator, the skipper seemed to be relaxed only in the company of one or two senior squadron officers. He seemed reluctant to join into informal conversation with a group of junior officers who were curious to find out what made the new skipper tick.

Thus was Jake Jacobson — a great young communicator who had the ear of Dave Davidson — sent to locate Dave and the skipper and to bring them "in about thirty minutes" to our little center of culture. The 30 minutes gave us time to prepare Marian, the librarian. She was truly one of God's great creations. Long of limb, true blonde, and heavily tanned, she was trim and athletic enough for the task at hand.

When the skipper, Dave, and Jake came through the door all neatly attired in military khaki, Dave and Jake stepped aside and allowed Marian a direct and unobstructed path to the target.

With a running start, Marian left the floor a good five feet in front of Swede, wrapped the longest legs in Westmoreland firmly around her target, placed slender velvety arms around the skippers "up-tight" neck and declared in her finest Oklahoma rancher's accent, "Swede dahlin', you is mine!"

The silence was so strong you could hear it. Swede Carlson, with frozen straight face, and without a word, managed to place Marian back on her feet without injury.

Then he sort of dusted his uniform with his hands before looking up. Staring at him, were all us ensigns holding our breath. Our faces were frozen into classic chicken-matter grins. We were suddenly and soberly aware that we might have torn it for good.

I remember searching Dave Davidson's face, but he seemed to be as much in the dark as us ensigns. Then Swede slowly looked each of us in the eye, allowed us to sweat just a little longer, then the first lines of a smile began. The smile grew and grew. His face became a great pleasant map of lines, some deep, some barely visible. They told us in no uncertain terms that we were in the presence of acceptance and appreciation.

"I think you fellows could use a little refreshment," were Swede Carlson's first informal words to us junior officers. Swede bought the first round and VA-195 went on to become, for my money, the best attack squadron in the United States Navy.

Yet, it is sad to admit that I was reluctant to write this little tale, even though it is true and caused no harm to anyone. Marian, if she is still around, would undoubtedly add that she enjoyed the hell out of her role.

Many things in our world have changed since those long ago nights in Westmoreland, California, when young pilots facing a new and unknown type of war captured a few moments of relaxation. One such happening has been "Tailhook," also a brief event, but one whose subsequent commentary can, if allowed, "make cowards of us all."

In September 1991 the Tailhook Association, which consisted of mostly Navy pilots, active and retired, who had landed an aircraft aboard an aircraft carrier, held their annual meeting at the Las Vegas Hilton. There was wide publicity that sexual harassment of several females had occurred. A Navy Investigation was conducted. As a result of public pressure the careers of many outstanding Naval Officers, some not present, were destroyed. The few that were guilty were not singled out in the press, but instead the entire Naval Air Establishment was branded as a sexually crazed and arrogant group.

Carrier pilots from the Korean War are no longer large in number, and they are no longer young. Some remain where they fought, or trained to fight, and where they died. Their bodies are now a part of long-forgotten places, but the transient nucleus that was them remains unclouded in the minds of those who remember.

Those of us still around are no longer totally naïve and we are not entirely carefree. Our optimism is often on standby, and our nonchalant swagger is sometimes more stooped than upright. It is probably also true that we are not quite so nice as once we were.

So there are days now — those when I am overly saturated with the latest of our world's fiascoes — when I am sometimes afflicted with a bad case of "the dumbs." When I feel such an onslaught approaching, I search my bag of experiences to choose an old and proven technique for escape. One is golf, but if that is not practical at the time, another effective remedy is to put my old worn copy of Michener's *Bridges* on the VCR. For then I am able to see again those big white "B's" on the tails of beautiful old aircraft and I am instantly engulfed with remembrance of another time. My mind is cleared of current commentary; it becomes flooded with the background sounds of many aircraft engines — some are beginning their noisy task, and others are winding down. Again, I can feel the roll and pitch of a flight deck and smell the marvelous clean musky air that can only be found on the open sea. I hear again the voices and see the faces of a bunch of great guys. They are doing important and exciting things.

Most of them are flying old propeller-driven ADs and Corsairs, but there also are Johnny Magda, Ray Hawkins, Ken Wallace, and other early carrier-jet pioneers, all in VF-191 at the time. They are flying straight-wing F9Fs — the Navy's first carrier jet — off the straight deck of the Princeton, writing those early exciting "learning curve" chapters regarding carrier-jet operations.

Our very best pilots today, flying off angled-deck carriers would do a quick double take if on their next flight they saw only a landing signal officer and a nylon barricade separating them from a pack of aircraft parked ahead. Straight-deck pilots were forced to do it right the first time. There was no going around if you missed a wire.

Quickly, before I am misunderstood, let me add that my grandfather, like many grandfathers before him, often said, "It was much tougher in our day."

Jets did change aviation immensely, but in 1950 the carrier jet was designed to carry light bullets, not heavy bombs; their job was to shoot down other aircraft, not dive-bomb large steel and concrete bridges. But due to the public's desire for vicarious experience, writers sometime resort to sensationalism, not fact.

Michener, in his writing, used jets that were designed as air-to-air fighters, to knock out bridges that required direct hits with extremely large and heavy bombs. In 1950 the AD, not a carrier-jet fighter, was the aircraft that could lift these bombs from the deck of an aircraft carrier and deliver them with precision to destroy targets such as those found in Swede Carlson's canyon.

So I watch the old tape again, searching for familiar faces, ignoring those parts that are not factual, and enjoying the remembrance. Soon I find myself able to return again to contemporary happenings with a smile. Again I am reminded that straight is straight, whether we speak of wings, flight decks, or truth. Dave Davidson, were he still around, would have no trouble with such elementary thought. "Just consider the facts and check your sources," he would say.

In *Bridges*, Michener inserted sensationalism for fact, all for the sake of entertainment. No real harm was done. Swede Carlson would no doubt have welcomed the opportunity to share a drink with Michener and point out to him, with a smile, how he screwed up.

But not so with "Tailhook." Here, not one but several people screwed up; then the media in a massive frenzy to out-do one another, substituted sensationalism for fact. A very great and serious harm was the result.

By failing to heed the common sense of the Dave Davidsons of our world and calmly separating the few who deserved punishment from the group as a whole, we allowed innuendo to tarnish the reputations of great people. We allowed rampant scandal to undermine a distinguished institution, senseless irresponsibility to endanger our country's security, distortion of truth to obscure a proud history.

We did all of these insane things for the actions of a very few. A few to whom Swede Carlson would not have offered a soda pop.

Chapter 10

The F4U Corsair in 1949 was an aircraft whose reputation for beauty and for killing ensigns was well established among Navy pilots. The long-nosed, short-winged, single-seat fighter was developed for air combat in World War II. It was a real hunk of aircraft. So that maximum power could be obtained from its huge engine, the propeller was enormous. This in turn necessitated long landing struts to prevent metal blades from striking the ground.

To keep the airplane from looking like an awkward long-legged bird, the engineers designed a gull shape into the wings so the landing struts could be shorter. The result was an aircraft that many believe to be the most beautiful ever built. But it was also an aircraft that was unforgiving of pilots who made mistakes. The blue monster would jump up and bite you with no warning whatsoever. The F4U demonstrated over and over that she had little compassion for pilots who did not follow her strict rules.

The short gull wings performed great when there was enough airspeed to provide abundant airflow over slick blue surfaces. But the F4U was built to be flown by Navy and Marine pilots, and that necessitated that it be designed to land aboard an aircraft carrier. This meant the pilot had to slow it down and hang the airplane on its huge propeller. In addition, the nose of the Corsair stuck out ahead of the pilot for half the distance of its length; and if you did not stay in your turn until the LSO gave you the cut, the nose would block his signals from view.

When the airspeed was slow, the stall speed of the wings was critical. Most airplanes — like the Cubs I had flown in Hillsboro and at Southwestern, and then the SNJ in Pensacola — give a nice buffeting feel before they stall and put the aircraft into a spin. This "courtesy" notice allows the pilot to add power, or if altitude permits, drop the nose, and gain airspeed.

But the Corsair gave little or no warning. When it stalled, it stalled. Unless the pilot had a lot of altitude, he was in serious trouble. The left wing dropped and if you added full power, which was the normal pilot reaction to keep from falling out of the sky, the Corsair would roll to the left and keep rolling so long as full power was applied. If you were close to the ground or water, you crashed. This could break up your day, and all of us scheduled to fly the Corsair were sternly warned that we were not to stall the F4U close to the ground.

After a few weeks of ground school, where we learned what made the F4U tick, we made our first flights. I remember the tremendous feeling of power during that first takeoff. My right leg muscles can still sense the huge amount of rudder pressure required to keep the nose headed straight down the runway. When I felt the wheels leave the runway, I raised the landing gear quickly. I had drummed this into my mind because so many guys forgot to do so on their first flight, and the Corsair looked just terrible with its landing gear hanging down, flying low and disappearing across farms and ranch land that surrounded the outlying landing field.

When I got to altitude, I trimmed the Corsair for straight and level flight so that the aircraft was practically flying itself. The long blue nose stretched forever ahead of me. I listened to the power of the enormous engine as it spun a propeller that pulled me through the beautiful morning faster than I had ever flown before. Then I dipped the wings to sense the quick response to control. And then I fell in love.

But it was a strange kind of love. I quickly learned to admire and respect the Corsair, and was proud to be in her company, but I never truly relaxed around her long enough to learn to trust her. It was like walking into a bar when you are lonesome for someone to talk with, and after a couple of drinks you find yourself in deep conversation with the best-looking girl in the place. You are happy and flattered that this great experience is happening, but you also sense that the beautiful seductive nymph smiling sweetly before you is also interested in every other guy in the place and will leave you in a New York second when the right opportunity comes along.

Once airborne and trimmed up, flying the F4U was comparable to steering a 1930s vintage Rolls Royce through the sky. The ride was like velvet. You had the sensation when moving the short stocky throttle with your left hand and controlling every movement of the aircraft with the stick in your right hand, with your feet placed firmly against the rudder pedals, that you were in control of something very special. You leaned backwards in a seat that was designed to help the human body withstand G-forces. Your legs were bent in front of you. The perception was comparable to driving a sports car — but sports cars cannot "slow roll" around puffy white clouds then loop toward the heavens with power to spare.

On those first landings we came over the end of the runway with plenty of speed. As the months went by, we gained confidence; and with lots of air space between us and the ground, we learned to fly the Corsair slow. We found out exactly where the stall speed was when the airplane was in all sorts of attitudes and configurations. Slowly and carefully we learned to hang the F4U on its propeller and stay about five knots above stall speed. This was the technique needed to land aboard a carrier, and after five months of flying the Corsair we became proficient enough to give it a go.

In all of my flying experience, which is more than most but much less than those who spent 20 or 30 years testing and flying the really hot stuff, I never had a more severe test of flying skill than landing a Corsair aboard an old straight-deck jeep carrier while in flight training. Later, in Korea, a small group of us developed a method to literally fly a 2,000-pound bomb into the mouth of a 17-foot railroad tunnel in mountainous terrain. That got my attention, but except for the fact that the bad guys were shooting at you and were not friendly if you wound up on the ground, the tunnel work was not much more involved than landing the F4U aboard a jeep carrier.

As the years go by, my admiration for the pilots who flew the Corsair in World War II and in Korea increases. Many of them flew Corsairs off the decks of our smallest carriers during combat operations. They did so for many months at a time. Sometimes the seas were rough. And sometimes the pilot, or the plane, or both, were shot all to hell. Then, at the end of the flight, when they were near exhaustion, they were required to execute a test of flying skill that required perfection. Their proficiency and endurance, day after day, month after month, never ceases to amaze me.

As I recall, our group of 21 Corsair students, three flights of seven, suffered five fatalities in six months. One was an engine failure, and the crash landing on the King Ranch near our base was not successful. Another of our buddies crashed into the water after a gunnery run on a towed sleeve over water. No one was certain as to what went wrong. The others were killed when they stalled the F4U at low altitude while landing.

We went back to Pensacola for carrier qualification and were based again at N.A.A.S. Corry Field. In 1949, even though the world was mostly at peace, Corry was a bustling place. During the years that stretched from the end of World War II until the Korean War every new Navy and Marine pilot passed through the gates of Saufley, Whiting, or Corry. All three training bases were close to Pensacola.

Today, the short runways of Corry Field are slowly disappearing as new buildings and grass take over. A Navy hospital stands nearby and a Navy electronics school occupies most of the old buildings. Sometimes my wife,

Annie, and I drive alongside the fence that borders the south side of Corry next to the road that heads out to "Fergi" Ferguson's little one-strip airport, where the Stagger-wing Beach that Fergi and I never got around to rebuilding still hangs from the ceiling. Along the way, I look at the small stretch of worn runway that still shows through the weeds, and I am reminded of a scene from the movie, *Twelve O'clock High*. In my imagination I do not see Gregory Peck, I see the faces of old friends. Many of them are gone now, but one or two are still around, and about once a year we meet at some Navy function. We have a few drinks, and tell a few lies, and remember some of the most exhilarating days of our lives.

Just six months before we reported aboard N.A.A.S. Corry Field to learn to fly the Corsair aboard a carrier, our class had been at the same place, living in the same barracks, eating in the same chow hall, learning to land the SNJ aboard the USS Wright. Now we were back. This time, to learn to land the F4U aboard the USS Cabot. The Wright and the Cabot were nearly identical carriers; their missions had been changed by the Navy.

But nothing had changed with Annie and me. While I was at Cabaniss Field, she visited my folks in Texas and we attended a very good class-twenty party in Corpus Christi. When I got back to Pensacola our adored 1935 Chevrolet was gone, so Annie and I dated using busses and taxis and borrowed automobiles. When we entered Corsair training, our group was promoted to Midshipmen First Class. Monthly pay did not increase but we were allowed more weekday liberties.

Some of our best dates were at the Rendezvous Club, a

battered barn of a building on the water in the old section of town. A black man named Wally Mercer led his own band, played a mean sax and sang, "Do the Hucklebuck." Phil Sanchez, Annie's father, not only knew everything that went on at the San Carlos Hotel, he also knew the entire town like the back of his hand. The Rendezvous was strictly off limits for his daughters, and that fact alone probably made our times there seem even better. In looking back, Phil no doubt knew everything we did, but he never said a word about it. Phil was in many ways like another father to me. We enjoyed a mutual understanding that was something special.

Our Corsair Class spent about a month at Corry. We lost another of our classmates in a gruesome landing crash near the main gate. But all in all, learning to land the Corsair aboard a carrier was very similar to the techniques we had learned in the SNJ.

On July 22, 1949, I made seven landings flying the Corsair aboard the USS Cabot. My feelings were comparable to the SNJ experience but different. I do not recall admiring the view of the water or the sky. I am positive that I had no inclination to push the mike button and tell everyone listening of my enthrallment. I only remember concentrating on holding my airspeed and altitude exactly where I wanted them. The airspeed was about 10 miles an hour above stall speed downwind. Then I slowed to no more than 90 knots during the approach and tried to hold it at an exact 85 knots as I neared the ramp. This gave me five knots above published stall speed, and I could only hope that the airspeed indicator had been calibrated on the money.

I kept the aircraft turning right up to the time I got the cut. As the Corsair approached the fantail (the rear end of the carrier), the Landing Signal Officer would level your wings and give you the cut in one fluid motion. In many respects the LSO was flying the aircraft for you. He would bank his paddles as he wanted you to bank your wings. He would stand on one leg and kick with his other when he wanted rudder. He would dip the paddles when you were low, raise them when you were high, bang them back and forth in front of him when you were slow, and drop one paddle to his leg when you were fast.

We spent many hours working with the same LSO at outlying fields before he waved us aboard the carrier. The LSO knew each of us and our flying abilities and habits better than we knew them ourselves. He knew when he could "cut" one pilot for landing and be confident that he would land safely and then on the very next approach give another pilot a wave off. He would do this even though both pilots had flown their aircraft into identical positions. The LSO knew his pilots so well that he knew the first pilot would correct before touchdown and that the second pilot probably would not.

I made seven landings without a wave-off when qualifying aboard the Cabot in the Corsair, not because I was perfect, but because the aircraft had my total respect and concentration. I was not giving an inch to chance.

Now, as I look back over my life, I sometimes wish that I had been able to give all matters that same intense concentration. It is a ridiculous thought and would have led to a miserable existence. But there were mistakes I made along the way that were due solely to my own indifference and insensibility — mistakes that I would never have made in July of 1949, when low over the blue waters of the Gulf of Mexico, flying the Corsair aboard the USS Cabot.

It was a routine close-air-support mission in the mountains of central Korea. A battle raged for control of one of the many hills that we had fought so hard to capture, and then to recapture. The fighting was intense. The tightness in the air-controller's voice told us that we were needed.

The hill was bare except for a few burnt stubs of trees. We could see trenches on both sides of the battle line. Using smoke flares, the controller directed us to the one that was our target.

I dropped all 12 bombs on one pass. The first of the bombs hit at the beginning of the long ditch packed with Chinese, North Koreans, or both — a congregation of enemy intent on killing our guys, if we did not kill them first. The remaining 260-pound fragmentation bombs walked down the center of the trench. The last sharp blast of shrapnel struck at the very end.

When I rolled the AD and looked back, there was nothing but a long line of dust and dirt where packed bodies had been. The controller on the ground pushed his mike, no doubt subconsciously, and spoke in a clear whisper, "Good God Almighty!"

High in the air, the same words had just flashed through my mind.

Chapter 11

The last glow of sunset added a touch of redness to the darkening sky behind the Golden Gate Bridge. Closer by, the lights of hundreds of cars crisscrossed the newer Bay Bridge, which pointed like an arrow to the heart of San Francisco. I was standing by one of the large windows in the ready room of VA-195, high atop a hanger that overlooked an airfield.

After completing Corsair training during the summer months, I received orders to the Naval Air Station at Alameda. The huge complex was snuggled against the shoreline across the bay from San Francisco. During World War II the base was a beehive of activity. Our largest carriers could dock next to the runways and load and unload an entire Air Group in record time. Alameda was the jumping-off spot for many Naval battles in the Pacific. Its docks have witnessed innumerable widows-to-be, waving to their loved ones for the last time.

On this early fall evening in 1949, however, Alameda was quiet. Below me on the darkening ramp were rows of Skyraiders, F4U Corsairs, and F8F Bearcats. All were assigned to Air Group Nineteen and were secured for the night. Gradually the lights of the City by the Bay became brighter and more golden as the last red glow vanished from a darkening sky. It was a stunning and beautiful sight, which would remain locked in my memory for many years to come.

On that special evening in 1949, most of the world was at peace. A cartoonist named Charles Schulz was working hard on a new comic strip named *Peanuts*, which would make its appearance the following year to compete with *Pogo* and *Lil' Abner*. Senator Joseph R. McCarthy was pushing the State Department for a conviction in the Alger Hiss case. Harry Truman was beginning to feel comfortable in his first year as an elected President. His unexpected defeat of Thomas Dewey the year before was still a subject for heated conversation. George Orwell's *1984* first appeared in bookstores and Arthur Miller's *Death of a Salesman* won the Pulitzer Prize.

An unknown starlet named Marilyn Monroe had just completed *Ladies of the Chorus*. Hollywood liked what they saw and she was now studying the script for another movie, to be called *Love Happy*. Elsewhere, the United States of America, with exemplary bureaucratic foresight, was hurriedly withdrawing the last of its occupying troops from a place called South Korea.

I was on duty for 24 hours as Squadron Duty Officer and wishing that I could be across the Bay at a bar called the Yankee Doodle. Several of the squadron's bachelors were there, sipping drinks, studying the crowd, and thinking of walking up the street to hear a little live jazz and checking out a different atmosphere.

After carrier qualification in the Corsair, our group had celebrated in Pensacola. Annie and I and several other couples ate fried chicken at Bartels, drank their wine, and then moved on to hear Wally Mercer's saxophone. Later we led the "Hucklebuck" conga line around the creaky floor of the Rendezvous.

Early in the evening Annie and the other girls had pinned our gold wings beneath the flaps of our shirt pockets so they could not be seen. The wings were not authorized for display until pinned on us later at an official ceremony in Corpus Christi. But after our last landing aboard the Cabot, as far as our Corsair class was concerned, it was all over but the shouting. We were fleet-qualified Navy Carrier Pilots.

Although of little significance to us at the time, we joined a group of pilots that would become more and more unique as the years rolled by. We had won our wings, but not our commissions as ensigns. We were Flying Midshipmen and would remain so until we completed a two-year contract.

By the time of the Korean War, there would be about 3,000 of us, and that is all there would ever be. At that time Congress appropriated funds for the restart of the Aviation Cadet Program and ended Admiral Holloway's Midshipmen program.

With the fall of evening and the quiet that prevails on a Naval Air Station after the securing of all aircraft for a weekend of liberty, there was ample time to think. My thoughts began to center on the past weeks of flying the AD.

After months in the Corsair, the AD was like switching

from driving a powerful sports car to what we now call a minivan. That, of course, is an exaggeration, but in the Corsair you sat leaning back in your seat with your knees high. Stretching far ahead of you was the long nose of the aircraft. In the AD you sat just behind a massive engine. You felt you could reach and touch the propeller. The vision was great. Everything was behind you. The engine was more powerful than the Corsair and the AD was a larger airplane.

The wings of the AD were long and thick. The tops were curved to form an airfoil that provided tremendous lift. There was a joke circulating at the time that the AD tailhook had a special lock so that it could not drop on takeoff. It was believed by some that there was a real danger that it might drag the carrier into the air.

But despite the enormous power of the AD, the pilot's great visibility while in the cockpit, the feel of the hydraulically boosted controls that gave positive and easy maneuverability, and its great stability during a landing approach, the AD felt to me more like flying a Cub than a powerful combat aircraft. I made the mistake of saying this out loud after my first flight and it came back to haunt me.

A few days later, my old roommate and good Texas buddy from preflight, R.R. "Railroad" Smith, was killed when he suffered target fixation and flew his AD into the bombing target at Fallon, Nevada. Just after the accident someone asked me, "Do you still think it flies like a Cub?" The person asking the question had been a close friend of Railroad; and, without thinking, asked from a feeling of sudden bitterness. His remark gave me cause for thought.

Then, a short time later we were doing field carrier landing practice, working with a Landing Signal Officer. I made several approaches dangerously close to the stall point. I felt that I had such control of the aircraft that I could ride it right on the edge and make a "roger pass" every time. But the LSO gave me hell. "Atkinson," he said, "the sooner you gain a little respect for the AD, the longer you will stay alive! It is not a damn toy."

That pretty well did it for me. Whereas the Corsair had killed so many ensigns that it had my highest respect before I ever saw the aircraft, the AD was winning an imposed respect from me. I still felt the thing flew like a Cub, but I kept my mouth shut and forced myself to treat it with the respect of a Corsair. The formula seemed to work.

When we got down to serious dive-bombing practice, I really fell in love. Most pilots at the time wanted to be fighter jocks — shoot down a hundred enemy aircraft, win the Congressional Medal of Honor, and marry Hedy Lamarr or Lana Turner (or at least date them long enough to establish a warm and personal relationship). I had no objection to achieving all of the above, and as a matter of fact would have been proud to do so, but I also wanted to be a great dive-bomber pilot. Somehow, as a kid who read a lot during World War II, I got the idea that sinking ships and knocking out large and important enemy targets was a lot more important than shooting down some airplane.

So when I discovered that the AD was the best propeller-driven dive-bomber ever designed, one of my big dreams came true. The thing had enormous "barn doors" — dive brakes that extended from each side and below the aircraft. They were nearly the size of barn doors, hence the name. During practice we rolled in about eight to ten thousand feet and came as near straight down as we could. The dive brakes held our speed low so that we felt as though we were hanging in the air. There was all sorts of time to pick out the target, trim the aircraft for the dive, and get the nose well below the target so the wings would pull forward into perfect position as we came down.

As the aircraft passed about 3,000 feet, the target was coming into position. It was just a matter of minor adjustments to place the bombsight exactly where you wanted it to be.

Flying from NAS Alameda in 1949, we dropped only small smoke bombs on nearby practice targets. The techniques we developed would later be used in Korea to knock out railroad bridges only a few feet wide. The AD, with only one engine and flying from an aircraft carrier, could carry a larger bomb load than a B-17 during World War II. Let it never be said that aircraft designers do not earn their money.

It was also during this period that we developed a technique that led to the shooting down of a Russian MiG by the huge, non-fighter AD. As sort of an afterthought, someone designed one 20mm cannon into each wing of the AD. We never practiced with the things, and little thought was given to bore-sighting them so that they shot straight, but the two guns were there, and in Korea we used them on occasion for strafing.

In late 1949 the Air Force was getting its first jets to operating squadrons. Some of the squadrons were located at Hamilton Air Force Base about 50 miles northeast of Alameda, not far from the Navy's practice bombing range. The Air Force "jet-jocks" liked nothing better than to jump a division of four ADs flying home from bombing practice. We soon developed a defensive technique. Whoever spotted the jets — they were usually high above setting up for a run — would call out to alert our flight. We were on a different frequency, so the jets never knew we had them in sight and were waiting. When the jets were close to firing position, our division leader would call out "Dive Brakes," then after a short pause, "Now!"

All four of us would extend our dive brakes at the same time and stay tight on the division leader as he turned sharply into the oncoming jets. It was the same as suddenly stomping hard on your brakes in 70-mile-an-hour traffic on an interstate highway. All the traffic whistles past you, and so did the jets. Then it was just a matter of "Dive Brakes In! Now!" as the division leader turned in behind the jets for a perfect shot. Using this technique an AD did shoot down a Russian MiG in Korea; and, using the same technique, my buddy, Dave Millpointer, came close on his second combat tour. I was then in another Air Group and did not see the happening, but Dave tells the story well. He was flying lead with two ADs and did all of the above just like we did in Alameda, except when he turned to line up and fire on the MiG, his wingman had gotten out of position and had slid his AD right in front of him. Dave screamed for his wingman to get out of the way, but the guy was confused, could not see Dave, and by the time Dave had a clear shot the MiG was well on its way to the Yalu River. Dave, when telling the story, let his voice become even more disgusted and sarcastic than when he leaned close and told the Army Colonel that his story was "goddamned fascinating!"

Sitting at the duty desk in Alameda on that quiet evening in 1949, I had no way of even guessing as to what lay ahead. I only knew that whatever it was, I was looking forward to the happening with excitement.

Four of us — Gootch, Red, Jason, and myself — shared room 117 aboard the USS Boxer from early January until the fall of 1952. Even now, nearly 50 years later, when it is just Annie and myself for cocktails, or on very rare occasions when Red Rumble and I get together, I sometimes feel the urge to sing a little ditty the four of us wrote during the early days of Air Group Two's tour aboard the USS Boxer. This was toward the end of the Korean War.

Like some of the crazy characters in the movie *M*A*S*H*, we also had crystal cocktail glasses stashed — not in a tent, but in our stateroom. On rare occasions we would mix a real martini, but usually it was just government-issue medicinal brandy after our return from flying a combat mission. We loved the martini glasses because we could make our toast, click the glasses, and then listen carefully for the nice resonant ring that followed. This gave us perfect pitch to harmonize our little masterpiece:

From the Cockpit

It's Cocktail Hour
In One Seventeen.
We Will Drink
Ting-a-ling
To You-u-u-u-u-u-u!

After the drink, Lester "Gootch" Johnson would near-ly always "poof" his empty miniature brandy-bottle. This was done by screwing the little metal top on the bottle real tight, then holding the miniature under hot water until the fumes built up pressure. Finally, placing his lighted Zippo at exactly the right spot, Gootch would remove the cap, and — "Poof!" — a streak of blue flame would shoot from the neck of the little bottle just like a small acetylene torch.

This always called for another verse. We would make only one small change.

We will POOF! … Ting-a-ling
To You-u-u-u-u-u!

It was in one seventeen that I accumulated a mental storage of Gootch stories. The first I remember is "Liverlips Dwyer."

Lester Johnson was the only "ring knocker" among us junior officers. He graduated from the Naval Academy toward the end of World War II and was ordered to duty aboard a cruiser headed for the Mediterranean. The war was over and Gootch was a junior division officer by the time he had his first liberty in Paris. Like any red-blood-ed and healthy young sailor, he partook most enthusiastically of nighttime Paris.

On his last night of liberty in Paris, Gootch got back to the Mediterranean coast so late that all the boats back to his cruiser had left. This resulted in paying for a small open rowboat to take him to his ship. The sea was heavy, and by the time the French sailor finally bounced the tiny craft against the gangway of the cruiser, Lester and his dress blue uniform were soaked with seawater.

The sky was now pink in the east, and sobriety had returned enough for Gootch to remember that Admiral's Inspection for all hands was at 8A.M. sharp. Privately, Lester referred to the Admiral only as "Liverlips." Suddenly, in his mind, Gootch could see a vivid picture: The Admiral's huge lips were snarled most unhappily while perusing his newest division officer's uniform.

Gootch quickly scampered up the gangway, gave a quick salute to the officer of the deck who was fighting hard to keep a straight face, and headed for his stateroom.

For the next three hours Ensign Lester Johnson did his best to restore his uniform. He squeezed out buckets of seawater, blotted the material with towels and pressed and pressed with his handy travel iron. Then he went to work on his black dress shoes. They were totally soaked and he kept adding coats of shoe polish until at last they again appeared to be shiny black.

At 7:30A.M. Ensign Lester Johnson stood spick and span in front of his division of 50 sailors, as a glaring Mediterranean sun began its brilliant trip across the morning sky. At 8A.M. sharp, Admiral "Liverlips" Dwyer began the personnel inspection of his flagship.

Unfortunately for Ensign Johnson, he started the inspection at the far end of the cruiser. For three hours Gootch stood in the dazzling brightness of a Mediterranean morning that became hotter with every passing minute. His eyes were focused straight ahead with only a slight glance now and then to track the inspection party.

At long last, Liverlips Dwyer was standing directly in front of Ensign Johnson. Gootch gave the admiral his snappiest salute and remained at attention. He could feel the admiral's eyes as they traveled up and down his uniform. Then he saw the snarl of thick lips.

Turning to the assistant who was taking the admiral's inspection notes, the admiral said: "I want to see this officer in my cabin immediately after inspection."

Gootch was dumbfounded. After three hours of hard work on his uniform, he felt that he looked as sharp as he had at any inspection he ever stood.

After the admiral was out of sight, Gootch took a quick look to see what was wrong. It only required a slight glance downward. His highly polished black shoes were now snow white. Not only white, they looked as though they were sprouting salt crystals. The long hours in the hot sun had baked the white salt to the surface of the seawater-soaked leather.

But luck oftentimes renders special good fortune to fools and drunks. The next week Ensign Johnson's request for flight training (which he had submitted after graduation from the Naval Academy) came through, and Gootch made his fast and most welcome escape from Liverlips Dwyer.

Chapter 12

Stoney Tennyson and I grew up 30 miles apart in central Texas, but I never knew him until he reported aboard VA-195 at NAS Alameda shortly after the Korean War began. Stoney had been a carrier pilot in World War II and was still a Lieutenant (Junior Grade) in 1950. Stoney always insisted that he was the oldest JG in the United States Navy and he just might have been telling the truth. He certainly looked the part, with streaks of gray showing in his thinning hair and a lean face crossed with tension lines.

The only explanation I ever heard for Stoney's being passed over for promotion to full lieutenant enough times to make him the oldest JG in the Navy came from Stoney himself. It was the first time a group of us went on liberty together in San Francisco.

We were at our favorite watering hole, The Yankee Doodle, on California Street. The booze was good and not overpriced, the customers were mostly military, and the waitresses were pretty. They were also knowledgeable about Navy pilots. That first late afternoon, when we got together after work with Stoney, there must have been a half dozen of us in our group. We were lucky enough to be served by Nancy, our favorite waitress. Nancy had been raised in a Navy family and she knew Navy routine. She also knew most of our group by name. We introduced her to Stoney. She flashed her great natural smile and gave him a firm handshake, but I noticed that she did a quick double-take and focused on Stoney's face a moment longer than was normal for Nancy.

We sipped our drinks and began a discussion of the day's happenings. Our squadron was working hard, getting ready to deploy for a combat tour in Korea. There was a lot of flying to be done. The word was already out regarding Stoney Tennyson's flying ability. He was solid as a rock and could hold his own in the air with any of us. We were now trying to figure out what made him tick on the ground. It was obvious right off that he was a quiet one. He was friendly enough but seldom spoke unless spoken to. His brief answers were often humorous and left you wanting to hear more. Stoney was the kind of person that most people like immediately and want to know better.

When Nancy served the second round, she paused in front of Stoney. She placed his drink carefully on the table in front of him, then looked him straight in the eye. Her face was glowing with keen interest in this newest member of our group.

"Stoney? Is that right?" Immediately, Nancy had Stoney's attention.

"Yes ma'am," replied Stoney in his best Texas drawl. "You've got it just right."

Then Nancy said, "Well, Stoney, I'm curious. I cannot

help but notice that you look mighty old to be a JG."

Stoney immediately dropped his smile. A serious and despondent expression took total control of his face. He dropped his head slightly and spoke in a soft voice, but clearly enough so that all of us at the table could hear him plainly.

"I lost a Registered Pub!"

Nancy immediately broke into laughter. The rest of us at the table joined in. It may have been true that Stoney Tennyson was passed over because he had signed for a confidential document and lost it, but if that were the reason, his was the only such case we had ever heard of in our years in the Navy. Neither Stoney nor anyone else in the squadron ever brought up the subject of his age again. We liked Stoney's answer just the way it was.

When we got to Korea, Stoney quickly established his reputation as a proficient pilot. He was the kind that just quietly got the job done and did not have much to say afterwards. Following a particularly long and tough month of combat, our squadron was sent for a few days of rest and recreation to a mountainside resort that required a long train ride. Up to this time, Stoney and I had not gotten to know each other well. During the train ride there was ample opportunity for several hours of drinking and talking and Stoney and I became well acquainted. He had grown up in Waco, only 30 miles from Hillsboro. The more alcohol we consumed the more we recalled our "Texan Training" during our growing-up years. As the hours went by, we recalled for our group the bravery of many heroic Texans at the Battle of the Alamo and Goliad, and slowly Stoney and I convinced each other all over again that Texans were special people. By the time we reached the rest camp, we had separated ourselves from the rest of our group. It was obvious from our buddies' cynical remarks that they did not hold Texas history in sufficient high esteem, neither did they appreciate the special qualities of the two Texans who were present.

When we departed from the train, a long walk remained to the hotel. It was quickly apparent that hotel management at our rest camp had made no arrangements to pick up a group of unannounced Navy pilots at 2A.M. on a cold March morning. There was little light from a fingernail moon, and thick snow covered the road and surrounding mountains. A thin coat of ice covered everything in sight. Walking would be tricky in our black dress shoes, so Stoney and I struck out ahead. We were determined to demonstrate to the group that when the going gets tough, Texans always lead the way.

After a long walk we could make out the lights of the hotel and the outline of a wooden bridge that crossed a mountain stream. Stoney stopped and leaned over the railing of the bridge to obtain a better view of the roaring torrent below. Before I could join him, Stoney toppled over the railing and into the freezing water.

Without a second thought, I climbed on top of the railing and jumped into the unknown to save my newfound bosom buddy. I landed beside Stoney uninjured and managed to drag him to the banks of the stream, although Stoney was trying desperately to push me away and shouting for me to leave him alone. I ignored his shouts and proceeded to try to pull Stoney out of the water, but the banks of the stream were covered with ice and we kept sliding back. All the time, Stoney was fighting against me and screaming for me to let him go, but I was bigger and stronger and was determined to save him.

Our squadron had been well briefed on the hazards of hypothermia. We knew that the human body could not last long in freezing water. After repeated efforts to pull Stoney up the slippery bank only to slide back into the water, I was certain that we would soon freeze to death if I did not take drastic action. It became clear to me that I would have to knock Stoney unconscious in order to save his life.

I held Stoney in position with my left hand and aimed carefully to make certain that I would hit him square on the jaw with my right. Much to my surprise, this only made Stoney more angry. He screamed at me even louder. So I hit him again and again, determined to land my knockout punch. Finally someone grabbed my arms and others pulled Stoney free. The remainder of our group had come to our rescue. They had heard Stoney's shouting and rushed to find out what was going on.

With Stoney Tennyson — the oldest Lieutenant (Junior Grade) in the United States Navy — incapacitated, Sandy Sanderson, another of our squadron's JGs, became the most senior officer in our group. Immediately, Sandy demonstrated those leadership qualities that would in later years take him to the rank of Vice Admiral and a reputation as one of the most outstanding officers in the United States Navy.

Sandy, after taking quick note of the situation, immediately gave a firm order. "Get 'Alamo' and 'Goliad' out of that water and up to the hotel." Such calmness and clear thinking under pressure was truly awe-inspiring. During the train ride Sandy had consumed about as much booze as the rest of us, but suddenly he seemed to be sober as a judge. With Lieutenant (Junior Grade) Sanderson in charge, the early morning staff at the hotel registered our group and issued room keys. Using blatant discrimination, they assigned Stoney Tennyson and me to a small, secluded room buried at the back of the hotel. The staff led us to our room with Stoney still shouting at me and using impolite language. By the time they closed the door to separate us from the hotel's carriage trade, I had begun to fire a few choice remarks back.

I can still remember clearly my drunken dreams that night. After climbing beneath the covers into a small bed, I managed to cover my head with a pillow to block out Stoney's cursing from the bed across the room. Over and over I saw the roaring mountain stream that raced beneath the small bridge and felt the freezing water when I landed next to Stoney. Then I rolled and tossed, feeling the room go around and around as I struggled to get Stoney up the steep frozen bank and out of the water. And over and over we slipped back, and then I would try again.

Stoney and I slept until late the next morning. With few words spoken between us, we showered, changed into warmer clothes, and went to the hotel restaurant for a late breakfast. We were both sober but suffered terrible headaches. Stoney had one small bruise on the side of his head where one of my knockout blows had glanced off.

We were both curious to find out exactly what had happened.

After a large breakfast that included a lot of black coffee and several aspirin, we walked out of the hotel and found the wooden bridge over the "roaring mountain stream." The stream was about ten feet wide and not deep enough to reach to our knees. The banks on the side were covered with snow and ice but were not more than chest high, about the same as the height of the bridge above the water. I was totally devastated. The hero's rescue that I had dreamed of over and over during my rolling and tossing was not at all what I had envisioned.

Stoney and I smiled at each other, and, without saying a word, we walked back to the hotel, found the bar and our buddies from the squadron, and joined them for a drink. Only a few sarcastic remarks were directed our way. Neither Stoney nor I responded and neither of us mentioned the state of Texas again.

After that first Princeton cruise Red Rumble and I were transferred to Air Group Two to return to Korea aboard the USS Boxer. Stoney Tennyson remained with Air Group Nineteen and deployed again aboard the Princeton. The Boxer and the Princeton were sometimes in liberty ports at the same time, and Red and I were able to join up with some of our old VA-195 squadron mates. By swapping sea stories, we were able to keep track of most of our buddies.

Later we learned that when VA-195 returned to the states, Stoney Tennyson volunteered to remain for a third combat tour in Korea with VA-195's replacement squadron. A short time later Stoney and his AD were blown out of the air at high altitude with a direct hit from a large anti-aircraft shell — a "black hue," we called them. Such hits at altitude were rare in Korea, but they did happen.

I often think of Stoney and sometimes study an old photo I snapped of him when we were aboard the Princeton. A cloth helmet covers the thinning hair, but the curious half smile is there along with the lines of an older man. After our trip to the rest camp, there never seemed to be another opportunity for more long talks with Stoney. I never did get to know him well enough to determine what made him tick. Stoney was a man with a lot on his mind, which he did not care to discuss with just anyone. I doubt that he ever did find that special person or thing for which he searched.

In Hillsboro old timers referred to such a person as "having an itch that they could not scratch."

I suspect that on occasion, old timers in Waco also used the same phrase.

In the fall of 1950 the Korean War was underway and waiting for reinforcements. VA-195, a Navy Attack Squadron, stationed in Alameda, California, was busy screening and training new pilots so that the squadron could be brought to combat readiness as quickly as possible and head overseas.

Dave Davidson, our executive officer, was one of the screeners. Dave, Jake Jacobson, and I had flown together in Dave's "Tiger" division on a lengthy Pacific cruise, which had ended just before the Korean conflict began.

The fourth member of our division had been transferred, and Dave was screening a few of the new pilots to find a well-qualified person to fill our vacant slot. One of the new ensigns was scheduled with Dave, Jake, and me for a routine night-training flight. Dave assigned the new fellow to fly his wing in my old spot, Jake flew section, and I moved to Jake's wing, the number four position.

Dave led our flight out of NAS Alameda and over San Francisco Bay so that we would have a good horizon and enough light for a practice rendezvous. Dave was not one to take a new ensign out over dark water, with no horizon, to practice what could be a very dangerous procedure.

"Don't practice parachute jumps! Save that for times when there is no other choice," was a thought often expressed by Dave to us junior officers. He planned our flight that night to make our practice as safe as possible.

We made our usual break and tail chase, and then Dave began a wide shallow turn so that we could turn inside and join back into formation. Jake left plenty of space between his aircraft and the new fellow. I trailed well behind Jake so that we could both keep an eye on the rookie.

As Number Two got close to Dave, Jake and I could tell from his wing lights that he had thrown up a wing. By doing so, he totally blocked his view of Dave's aircraft. However, Dave, the wise old veteran, was on guard and moved his AD in time so that the new guy went screaming by. Number Two's Skyraider was on its side, the left wing pointing straight down and the right wing straight up. There was no way the new pilot trying to join on Dave's wing could have the slightest idea as to where Dave's aircraft was.

All in all, the try-out by the new guy was not off to a good start.

Dave called on the radio in a calm voice and said very simply, "OK, Number Two, let's try it again. Do not throw your wing up. If you have to, just slide on past me, but do not block me out."

Slowly the flight rejoined and Dave led us into another practice rendezvous. This time it was worse. Number Two came barreling into Dave at high speed, then stood his AD on its left wing, totaling losing sight of Dave's aircraft. Dave made a last-second fast climb, barely in time, and Number Two went scurrying past again. It was so close that Jake and I both thought the new guy had caught Dave with his wing.

Dave kept his patience, gave the new guy time to orient himself, and then to make a very slow join-up. Then Dave called, "OK Tiger flight, let's close it up and head for the barn." We had not been in the air thirty minutes on what was to have been a two-hour flight.

We landed, secured our aircraft, and headed for the ready room. Number Two was the last to enter and Dave Davidson was waiting. Dave took a hard look at the newcomer, studied him carefully, and then asked to see his goggles. Number Two's goggles had lenses that were so dark they looked black. In those days we had plastic lenses that fit into rubber goggles so we could change shades as needed. In bright sunlight we used a very dark lens and at night we used a clear one.

Dave studied the dark goggles. The lenses were the darkest made — they were designed for flying in the tropics. "Why are you wearing a daylight lens? Where is your night lens?" Dave asked in a voice that expressed his total disbelief in what he was seeing. We all observed the expression of nonchalance and total conviction on the new ensign's face.

"Well, you see, sir, by wearing the dark lens while night flying I have no trouble with night landings. When I am ready to land, I simply lift my goggles and everything is just like daylight." The newcomer seemed very proud of his keen insight into such an elementary problem.

Next morning the new ensign was no longer assigned to our squadron. Not long afterward, Dave Millpointer auditioned and became a great number four man in "Tiger" division. I moved back to my old number two slot, and we were ready for Korea. Dave Millpointer, like Jake Jacobson and myself, became a Dave Davidson disciple. We were just your run-of-the-mill common sense guys. But sharp enough to wear dark lenses in daylight and clear ones at night.

Chapter 13

Springtime 1950 in the Pacific was quiet, serene and nonviolent. Pacific, one might say. Manila Harbor, still littered with sunken ships from World War II, was a picture of tranquility. Many old warship superstructures, rusting and battered monuments to some of history's most ferocious naval battles, rose proudly above the shallow waterline. Silent.

Large landing craft, converted to liberty boats, crisscrossed the huge bay. At night they were packed with singing and carefree sailors. Happy seafarer sounds tracked the bulky old vessels across the harbor. Bit-by-bit the boisterous and melodious clamor was hushed to calming silence by long yellow-green phosphorus trails. The wakes stretched behind the moving craft and left a congenial pattern of brightness across shadowy darkness.

For a short interval that spring, the USS Boxer, one of our largest aircraft carriers, and the HMS Triumph, a smaller British carrier, both operated out of Manila. History was soon to record that the spring of 1950 would be the conclusion of a brief few years of serenity between wars — a good time for joint air operations with old friends.

The two carrier groups picked an untroubled day with perfect sea. A flight of four F8Fs from the Boxer made landings aboard the much smaller British carrier. On the same day, four British Fireflies flew to the Boxer for practice carrier operations. Many of us pilots on the Boxer were packed on "vultures row," a great viewing spot high in the island structure, from which we could observe the entire flight deck. From there we could see every detail of the landings by the British.

The first three British planes landed beautifully and taxied forward. The fourth made a near roger pass, took a cut in perfect position, then proceeded to float all the way to the barricade. Just a few feet higher and he would have gone completely over the heavy nylon straps that could stop an aircraft in flight. Had he done so, he would have crashed into the assembly of aircraft parked forward.

Fortunately, the wheels of the Firefly caught the top of the huge barrier and the aircraft was flipped to an abrupt stop. The pilot, uninjured, was pulled from the cockpit. Before going below, he looked up to observe our gallery of gawking faces, gave us a little wave and flashed a big carefree smile.

Later in the wardroom, several of us who had watched the British landings were seated around a large, green-felt-covered table. We sipped quietly from heavy mugs of steaming coffee and listened.

The other three British pilots — the ones who had made perfect landings on the Boxer — questioned their buddy as to what could have happened. After hundreds of successful landings on small British carriers, he had just fouled up a landing on one of the largest carriers in the world.

The pilot who had crashed sported a very heavy red beard, which he kept neatly trimmed. He was a seasoned lieutenant with Battle of Britain experience. He grinned from behind his heavy mask of red whiskers; his sunburned face was a mixture of lines, caused both by heavy stress and hearty laughter.

"Well, you see, mates, I knew I was in good shape, then I took the cut and looked ahead. These Yanks build things so bloody big, you know. There was just a whole lot of landing room ahead of me — like a nice pleasant stretch of runway back home — so surely you can understand, there was simply no urgency to rush the situation."

Such an uncomplicated explanation seemed to satisfy "Red Whiskers'" flying buddies. As for us ensigns, we just smiled, kept quiet and sipped coffee. Who could argue with such logic?

We were returning late from a mission one afternoon sometime during the Korean War. I cannot remember if it was during the first deployment when I was with VA-195, or during the second when I was with VA-65. Who I was flying with also escapes my memory. It could have been that Dave Davidson and I were flying alone, but that seldom happened; and Dave is now dead so there is no checking there. Neither of the other two members of our old "Tiger"division" in VA-195 remembers the incident, so I suspect that the event that sticks so clearly in my mind happened during the early months of 1952, when I was flying from the USS Boxer with Air Group Two.

Our flight heard the "Mayday" call, and finally we were able to locate two Corsairs close to the water. The one that ditched had been hit by antiaircraft fire and had made it to the water, headed for the carrier, when his F4U finally gave up and the engine stopped. Whoever the pilot was did a beautiful job of executing a textbook-perfect water landing. We were close by then, and from above we could see the pilot exit from the cockpit, climb out onto the wing and jump into the sea before the Corsair sank. It could not have been done better, even on a beautiful June day in the Gulf of Mexico. Unfortunately, the Corsair did not ditch in such perfect surroundings. The day was bitter cold, with a strong wind, and the sea-state was high. The water temperature was near freezing.

But the pilot had been unusually calm and collected, and when he knew the Corsair was near the end of its battle to get him home safely, he picked out the only small island in the area. He landed his stricken aircraft not more than the length of two football fields from the island. Two hundred yards is not a great distance for a good swimmer, and I suspect that the pilot of the Corsair was as good a swimmer as he was a pilot. At the time the Corsair pilot ditched, his wingman was talking with a rescue helicopter on its way from the carrier. The helicopter was still a good fifteen minutes out.

We watched as the pilot inflated his May West life preserver, jumped into the Sea of Japan, and began swimming. He did not make it halfway to the island before he disappeared below the waves. The pilot was probably wearing what we called a "Poopy-Suit." It was made of a thick rubber-like material and covered the entire body in a cocoon-like manner. Poopy-Suits sometimes leaked, and, when filled with water, they could drag a pilot and his fully inflated May West below the surface.

Flight surgeons gave estimates of 10 to 20 minutes in near freezing water before hypothermia would render a person unconscious.

Whatever caused the Corsair pilot's death that day, Poopy-Suit, hypothermia, or both, it was not the fault of the doomed Corsair pilot. It remains in my mind as another of those tragic events that just seem to be a part of war. Pilots and others like to think that when they do everything right they will live. But sometimes they just don't.

I now understand the tomb dedicated to the memory of an Unknown Soldier much better. The Corsair pilot who drowned that cold day in the Sea of Japan has become in my own mind a tomb to the unknown Korean War dead. Like many other "old soldiers," I remember many who died in combat. With most, I can put a face and a personality with the memory. But for all those others who remain nameless, the Corsair pilot comes to my mind. When my final moments come, I truly hope that I can go with the same grace and style that an unknown pilot demonstrated to all of us who looked down that long-ago day.

Chapter 14

Beginning in late June of 1950, the Korean War progressed from a retreat by United Nations forces from the 38th parallel to a foothold along the Pusan perimeter. Then in the fall came General Douglas MacArthur's highly successful Inchon invasion — to be followed in November and December by hundreds of thousands of Chinese troops storming south from Manchuria. Soon the 38th parallel was again the focal point for a bitterly fought struggle.

By March of 1951, Air Group Nineteen was busy knocking out railroad and highway bridges. They also strafed and rocketed truck convoys and trainloads of supplies that moved along narrow roads and rail lines through snow-covered mountains and frozen valleys. Under cover of darkness, military supplies from the north were moved south by train, truck, ox cart, and backpack. At the same time hundreds of North Korean and Chinese workers were busy laying rail lines over frozen riverbeds where large steel bridges had been bombed the day before.

Lieutenant Frank Metzner was Officer-in-Charge of a

VC-35 detachment aboard the USS Princeton. He and four other pilots who flew the night interdiction version of the AD hung their flight suits in our ready room. They were not members of our squadron, but we mingled as though we were all in the same family. And we were, except that Frank and his group flew mostly at night, and VA-195 flew in the daytime.

Frank Metzner was an interesting guy. After duty as a carrier pilot in World War II, he returned to civilian life and became a writer and radio announcer. He was, in effect, a communicator of ideas. From this relatively safe environment, Frank was suddenly recalled to active duty and soon found himself in Korea flying an AD from the deck of a carrier into pitch-black darkness. VC-35's mission was night interdiction. Using eyesight and radar, Lt. Metzner and his pilots searched. When they located a moving string of lights, they lit up the sky with tracers, rockets and exploding bombs.

After such a night, when morning was just beginning to emerge as a pink glow in the east, Frank and his wingman spotted several trains headed for nearby snow-covered mountain tunnels. Frank headed for one tunnel and his wingman for another. They both waited for trains to emerge. No trains reappeared. Apparently, the North Koreans were hiding them in the tunnels during the day.

While flying back to the carrier that cold March morning, Frank Metzner had an idea. He discussed it with his wingman, while walking from their aircraft across a rolling flight deck toward a routine intelligence debriefing. They both concurred that Frank's plan just might work. The result was a meeting with Rear Admiral Ralph

Ordnance man checks bomb load on VA-195 AD, April 1951, USS Princeton, Korea.

*Carrier Air Group
Commander, Air Group
Nineteen, Richard C.
Merrick, Korea, 1951.
Just one more day and
he would have made it
home.*

*Art Downing, Commander Air
Group Two (l.), and Bob Rich,
VA-65, relax aboard the USS
Boxer, June 1952, following
Suhio hydroelectric plant strike.*

*Skipper Swede Carlson. Commanding Officer VA-195,
USS Princeton, 1951.*

"Red" Reidl (l.) and "Red Dog" Thomas, USS Boxer, spring 1950.

Harry White, Commanding Officer, VA-195, USS Boxer, Southwest Pacific, spring 1950. After he put the first torpedo into the Battleship Yamato, during World War II, all the paint was burned from the front of his TBM. All Harry could recall of his torpedo run was solid flashes of fire just in front of him.

Hap and Ann Harris at Russian River, fall 1950.

Relaxing at Russian River, October 1950. (l. to r.) Hap and Ann Harris, Annie Atkinson, Don and Dee Monday.

Bob Bennett (l. front), Hap Harris (behind), Tommy Thomson (center), and Don Van Slooten (r.). "Boy's Town" entertainment, USS Boxer, Southwest Pacific, spring 1950.

Pat Murphy, former Blue Angel and VF-191 pilot, Korea, 1951. After Frank Soberski was blinded by enemy gunfire, Pat flew wing on Frank guiding him to a safe landing aboard the USS Princeton.

Chuck O'Reilly, Korea, 1951. He won dog fight with an Air Force Thunderjet while on his first jet flight, making good use of the Blue Angel logo and intimidation.

Frank Metzner, Korea, 1951. Officer in Charge of VC-35, he convinced Rear Admiral Ofstie to approve the "tunnel busting" concept to knock out enemy supply routes.

John Koelsch, helicopter pilot USS Princeton, 1951. John was awarded the Congresional Medal of Honor for bravery during the action that led to his capture.

*Dave Davidson,
Executive Officer VA-195,
"Tiger Division," May
1951, USS Princeton,
Korea.*

*"Gootch" Johnson aboard
the USS Boxer, 1952 off
Korea.*

VF-24 Panther, Air Group Two, flying from the USS Boxer over North Korea, June 1952.

*Stoney Tennyson, VA-195, USS Princeton, 1951. The oldest
Lieutenant (junior grade) in the United States Navy.*

*VF-191 Panther Jet ready to catapult from USS Princeton on Air
Group Nineteen's first day of combat in Korea, Dec. 5, 1950.*

Snow covers the flight deck of the USS Princeton, off the coast of Korea, December 1950.

Passing under the Golden Gate, 1950.

Frank Soberski, blinded by anti-aircraft shell fragments, after successfully landing his jet aboard the USS Princeton, May 10, 1951. Pat Murphy guided "Sober" to a safe landing.

Morgan Wilbur's painting depicts a VA-195 AD during a Korean War "tunnel busting" run.

VA-195 Skyraider aircraft knock out the Dam at Hwachon using World War II torpedoes.

Sandy Sanderson inspects battle damage to his VA-195 AD Skyraider, March 1951.

*VA-195 pilots (l. to r.) Bob Bennett, Sandy Sanderson, Gene
Sizemore, Marvin Quaid, Skipper Swede Carlson, Tex Atkinson,
Jake Jacobson, Phil Philips, and Jack Everling being honored at
Oshkosh in 2001.*

*USS Boxer explosion, August 5, 1952.
A bad day at sea. A sad day for many.*

Don Van Slooten,"Vulture's Row," USS Boxer, Southwest Pacific, spring 1950.

Hap Harris (l.) and Don Van Slooten, VA-195 Ready Room, USS Princeton, January 1951. Shortly before Hap's last flight.

Hap Harris, USS Princeton, January 1951.

Ofstie, Commander of Task Force 77, flying his flag aboard Princeton.

Their proposal to the admiral was to develop a technique to fly a large bomb with a delayed fuse into the mouth of a railroad tunnel. Although the plan was simple enough in concept, the admiral was skeptical. First, the bombing aircraft would have to come in low and slow, right on the ground, and would be a sitting duck for guns placed near the tunnel's entrance. Second, the largest of the North Korean tunnels was only 17-feet wide, and it was doubtful that such accuracy could be achieved with consistency.

Lt. Metzner was ready with answers. Four F4U Corsairs would lead every run, strafing the hills surrounding the mouth of the tunnel. Only ADs would be used for bombing. They could carry up to three 2000-pound bombs, using inboard wing and centerline racks, and they had sufficient power to clear the mountain after the drop. Most important, they were a very stable bombing platform. As to accuracy and consistency, a test of the concept would provide the answer. The Admiral gave Frank the OK to "give it a try."

I first learned of the project when VA-195 pilots were told the basic idea and asked to write their thoughts on how it should be done. We submitted our recommendations and then flew a test strike to see if our concept would work. Most of us came up with the same conclusion: Fly low along the tracks leading to the tunnel entrance, then release in time to clear the mountain. On our first hop, many of us dropped too soon while flying too fast. The result was a bomb that hit the railroad track short of the tunnel and bounced high. In one instance a bomb flew completely over the mountain that encased the tunnel and exploded just as it struck a bridge on the other side. In another, a Corsair pilot wound up flying wing on a bomb that could have exploded at any time.

But we learned quickly. We slowed the AD down, often using partial flaps, and made, in effect, a wheels-up carrier landing approach. I learned to line the AD up on the railroad track as far out as needed, then fly right off the deck straight for the mouth of the tunnel, slowing the AD to near landing speed. The tricky part was to remember which station was releasing the bomb. If off the right station, we lined up a little left — to fly the bomb, not the nose of the aircraft — to the center of the tunnel; if off the left station, vice versa. When dropping from the center bomb rack, we flew the nose of the AD dead center to the tunnel entrance then dropped a few feet high, because the center rack fired the bomb down to clear the propeller when in a vertical dive. Then immediately after release, it was full power and nursing the AD up and over the mountaintop, milking the flaps up as speed increased.

Soon after the test, Dave Davidson, our squadron executive officer, whose wing I had flown for over a year, told me that I would be flying with VC-35 for a while — as a tunnel buster. From March until May of 1951, VC-35 and VA-195 pilots flew many tunnel strikes. Most of my flights were with Lt. Atlee Clapp, who led our division of four ADs. Atlee was an outstanding pilot, well seasoned in World War II. He was the first of us to put a 2000-pound bomb inside a tunnel. We had started with 500-pound bombs, then 1000, then 2000.

When Atlee's 2000 pounds of deadly destruction exploded, I had a ringside seat. The tremendous force contained within the walls of the narrow tunnel drove dirt and debris out the other side much farther than the length of a football field. It struck me at the time that I had just witnessed the largest cannon shot in history.

Now, more than 50 years later, I still have vivid memories of our tunnel experiences. I recall one day when a runaway locomotive, pulling only the coal car behind, suddenly came dashing out the end of a tunnel following a huge explosion inside. All of us began chasing the locomotive, strafing away. We quickly determined that the runaway was unmanned, going full speed with a wide-open throttle. Our strafing was not having much effect, and we were thinking of bombing the railroad ahead when again, as often happens in such situations, some analytical mind in the group started thinking. He flew a few miles ahead and called to tell us to stop the strafing, that the runaway was headed straight for a crowded rail yard. So we pulled up, relaxed, and watched one of the most spectacular train crashes you could hope to see. Locomotives and boxcars flew in all directions. We watched from above with excitement, as though we were back home at a football game and our team had just scored a touchdown. After a few shouts, the dust settled and we flew on to our next tunnel.

By this time our tunnel-busting team was putting over 50 percent of our bombs into our targets. A flight of four ADs carrying 12 bombs, with four F4Us from VF-192 and VF-193 flying cover, could expect to knock out two or three tunnels during one four-hour mission. The Corsairs kept any antiaircraft fire in check. There was only occasional damage to an F4U or an AD — and no fatalities.

Such an operation would not work today. In most war zones it would be suicide. But it worked in 1951 and could have been used more extensively. Battle reports from the period contain little discussion of tunnel-busting and no valid explanation as to why the flights were discontinued.

Pilots doing extensive combat flying become a breed all their own. They live daily with life and sudden death, and soon develop their own set of values as to what is important and what is not. Most are quick to criticize the reasoning powers of coffee drinking "thinkers" on admiral staffs. When the tunnel operation was cancelled, those of us who had done the flying simply crossed it off as another instance when we were done in by staff thinkers. Most of us knew that if we remained in the service, we too would someday be sitting behind a desk thinking, not flying, but we did not hesitate to state our opinions concerning many staff decisions. We summed it all up in one simple statement: "When staffers find something that works, they quickly stop that operation and go searching for something new to try." So we went back to our old jobs — knocking out bridges and supply routes, and providing close air support for the troops.

Following his Korean duty, Frank Metzner chose to remain in the Navy. After returning stateside, he continued writing in his spare time, and, toward the end of the war, *The Saturday Evening Post* published Frank's article, "I Fly the Night Skyraider." In the article he recalls many hair-raising stories of night flying in Korea.

Frank was killed a short time later, while flying a summer orientation flight with a Naval Academy midshipman in Corpus Christi, Texas. The wings came off their SNJ Texan during a loop. When I heard the story, I recalled a day when Frank and I and several other pilots from our tunnel-busting team were watching films from F6F Hellcat drones that were attempting to do a job similar to ours. The drone had a forward-facing camera. Equipment in the controlling aircraft recorded the picture, as the drone — loaded with a 500-pound bomb — flew to the target.

When the F6F rolled in and pointed toward the target, all looked normal. As the drone got lower, those of us viewing in the darkened ready room sensed that we were flying the drone, watching the target get closer and closer. Then as the F6F dove below 1,000 feet, the ground appeared dangerously close. When the drone passed 500 feet, the target suddenly jumped up and slapped us in the face. The lights came on and everyone in the room was in a cold sweat. No living pilot had ever seen what we just saw, except on film.

I wish I could have spoken to Frank during those last few seconds near Corpus Christi, as he watched a live replay of that 1951 day in the ready room aboard Princeton. I would have told him, "Frank, you did good! Your skill in selling the tunnel-busting concept to Admiral Ofstie helped stop the delivery of tons of enemy ammunition. Some of those tons would have found their targets. Your abilities saved the lives of many a soldier who otherwise would have been buried in the dirt, in the snow and ice, and in the freezing waters of Korea.

Most of those who flew in Korea witnessed the last moments of some fellow airman's life. In most cases it involved an aircraft falling, with the doomed pilot watching the ground come up to slap him in the face, just as Frank Metzner had. Although it is seldom discussed among pilots, even during the most intense conversations, I suspect that many have wondered, just as I have, what flashes through your mind in those last few seconds. The closest analogy I can recall, when a pilot lived to tell his story, is that of Dale Faler when he was shot down in Korea. Dale became conscious just before crashing. He said that he recalls muttering, "Well, Dale, I guess we are going to die." Then he quickly answered himself, "To hell with that!" After a moment of frantic struggle, Dale bailed out and lived.

Many who were shot down in Korea were not as lucky as Dale Faler. They died, many of them instantly, and they took the remainder of their lifetime with them. At their funerals and memorial services, we heard orators speak of their heroic actions and sacrifice for country — all beautiful tributes to their memories. These things are true. But I doubt seriously that those who died like Frank Metzner used any of their final seconds thinking of the Korean War and of the millions in South Korea who would live better lives because of their bravery and sacrifice. My guess is that those who did not have the luck of Dale Faler died with thoughts similar to Dale's, "To hell with this!" They wanted to live; most had a lifetime ahead of them. They longed to hold a loved one just one more time, for long quiet talks with those who were most important in their lives. And no doubt in that last moment there was before their eyes a special and beautiful face, smiling in anticipation of all their tomorrows together, which now would never be. But who knows.

"Midshipman Atkinson, You've got it!"

Our Lieutenant (Junior Grade) instructor climbed into his jeep and raced across the small Naval Auxiliary Field near Corpus Christi, Texas.

I was left with a real mess that required sound command decisions. Balanced precariously on a bent and dirty four-bladed propeller, its tail climbing through small limbs of surrounding trees, was a Corsair that looked as though it might fall forward onto its back at any moment.

Still strapped in the cockpit was a member of our 1949 F4U class — white-faced. My eyes, and most certainly his, were focused on a huge tree stump. The jagged end was four or five feet high, left for some unknown reason when the land was cleared years before. Thinking in total silence, my classmate and I both calculated that if the Corsair completed its fall forward, the stump would hit the cockpit dead center. I quickly make my first command decision and issued my first official order: "Don't move!"

Sadly, both words of that first command were totally wasted. My classmate was already frozen. He was not moving a muscle. The well-worn "Hosenose," rocking gently in the strong Texas wind, managed to stay perfectly balanced.

It had been my turn to take notes for our instructor,

while others in our class made their first flights in the Corsair. My classmate landed in fair shape, but when he added power to take off for a "touch-and-go," the Corsair took charge and turned left. The out-of-control F4U spread a trail of dust that led directly toward a small patch of trees. The instructor and I jumped into his jeep and gave chase; we used the vehicle's radio to call for a crash truck.

For some reason, either communications or mechanical, there was a problem getting a crash crew to the scene. After the Corsair came to rest, our instructor carefully reviewed the situation, shouted instructions for the student to turn off all switches, and raced away in his jeep to get help. I remained with my first command.

In a short time a heavy truck arrived. Aboard was a tough-looking chief boatswains mate and several men who seemed to know what they were doing. Without a word from me, a ladder was quickly put into place. One of the men, using heavy rope, secured the tail of the Corsair to the strongest tree. Another boatswain then rescued my classmate.

About this time another jeep arrived to take my classmate and me back to join the rest of the flight. Turning to the chief boatswain, I mustered my newly acquired voice of authority.

"You've got it, Chief!"

I thought I saw the slightest flicker of a smile, but at such moments one can never be absolutely sure. The excitement of that first sensation of swift and total authority can sometimes blur reality and leave in its wake only irresponsible assumption and imagination.

Chapter 15

Some stories just stick in your mind the way you want to remember them — you do not want to be confused later by other versions. This is the situation, as I begin to tell you about "Red" Reidl and Harry "Red Dog" Thomas. On the Princeton cruise in Korea, the two Reds were flying Corsairs in VF-193 when I was flying the AD in VA-195. No doubt we flew together at times, and we had gone through training about the same time, but I did not get to really know them until after the war.

During the second cruise in Korea, I was in VA-65 aboard the USS Boxer and the two Reds were still in VF-193 for their second Princeton cruise. It was on this cruise that Red Reidl was shot down. I remember him coming aboard the Boxer to brief Air Group Two on survival techniques. This was pretty much standard procedure for carrier groups operating in Korea. Pilots who had been shot down and lived to tell their stories were interesting speakers. What they said could save your life.

I remember Red Reidl telling about bailing out of his Corsair and landing in an area of North Korea that was swarming with enemy troops. Red quickly gathered up his chute and buried it in mud beneath a group of trees. He then buried himself in the same mud. "Red Dog" Thomas was on the same flight, and he and the remaining Corsairs immediately began strafing runs to hold off the enemy soldiers who were moving toward the area where they saw the chute go down. Red Reidl got his survival radio working and was able to direct the flight to the nearest of the enemy troops.

Red was shot down late in the afternoon, and Red-Dog Thomas and the remaining Corsairs soon had to leave to return to the carrier. Red-Dog assured Red that the flight would return at dawn with a helicopter. Reidl dug himself in for the night and listened as enemy soldiers came closer and closer. Red was able to get his .38 pistol from its holster and be ready for morning.

Harry Red-Dog Thomas and a flight of Corsairs and AD Skyraiders were back at dawn, but it had not been easy. Red-Dog had a tough time convincing his senior officers that the mission had a chance of being successful. Finally, the rescue mission was approved, and on arrival they established radio contact and assured Red Reidl that a helicopter was on its way. Then the rescue aircraft began their strafing runs.

During the long night, Reidl had listened as enemy soldiers came close enough for him to reach out and touch. When the strafing began, he shot the closest soldier with his pistol. The tremendous noise of the aircraft zooming overhead blocked the sound of Red's shot. During each of the next four strafing runs, Red Reidl shot another soldier. When the helicopter arrived, Reidl was able to run and get into the sling without injury. Quickly the hoist began to jerk Red to safety. Reidl was proud of his record of five enemy soldiers in five shots and he had one shot left. As he was being hauled upwards, Red took careful aim, fired again, and missed. I can remember well his grinning to our group aboard the Boxer and saying, "It was that lousy helo pilot. He was ruff as a cob."

That is the way I remember Red Reidl telling the story, but some of my buddies say I am all screwed up. They say Red hid in a cave that was covered with spider webs to discourage the enemy troops from coming inside. They also say it was another pilot who emptied his .38 during the helicopter rescue. Whatever, I'm sticking to my story. The last time I saw Red Reidl he was still smiling. He was enjoying himself at a party with a beautiful girl he had just married. Red's buddies referred to her as Big Daddy's daughter from Mississippi. Red died early of a heart attack. I like to remember him laughing with his new bride and drinking mint juleps to the very end.

After the Korean War, Harry Red-Dog Thomas and I instructed in the same training squadron near Corpus Christi, Texas, for three years. We flew together often and became great friends. Later, when I heard that Red-Dog was killed in Vietnam, it really upset me. Harry had become skipper of a jet A4 Skyhawk squadron flying from a carrier. He was on a low-level mission when his aircraft was struck with antiaircraft fire and quickly crashed. There was no need for a rescue flight the next morning.

Shortly after the Korean War broke out in June 1950, the Navy's Blue Angels were given a new set of orders. Their scheduled air shows were cancelled and the team was transferred to become part of Air Group Nineteen at NAS Alameda. They flew their F9F jet aircraft from Texas to California, still with sparkling Blue Angels paint jobs, and parked them at NAS Moffett Field south of San Francisco Bay, because the runways at NAS Alameda were too short to handle jet aircraft comfortably.

The Blue Angel's skipper, Johnny Magda, an Ace from World War II, became commanding officer of VF-191. Other Blue Angels who joined 191 at that time were Jake Robcke, Pat Murphy, Fritz Roth, and another well-known Navy Ace, Ray Hawkins. Members of Air Group Nineteen, particularly us junior pilots, were suddenly conscious of a feeling that we were rubbing shoulders with future legends.

Those of us who were AD pilots in VA-195 could only hunger to fly a hot new jet, particularly one with a shiny Blue Angel logo for all to see. The pilots in VF-191 not only had the opportunity, but orders, to transition from their propeller-driven F8F Bearcats to jet-powered F9F Panthers.

Nineteen-fifties naval aviation was more informal than it is today. Pilots from World War II were in abundance, and the methods they had developed of necessity during combat conditions were still widely used. Reading the handbook for a new aircraft, kicking the tires, and uttering some colorful remark such as, "Let's give her a go!" were frequent occurrences. In several instances VF-191 Bearcat pilots used a similar procedure when they transitioned to the F9F jet.

Chuck O'Reilly was an ensign in VF-191 when the Blue Angels suddenly became part of his squadron. Air Group Nineteen had just returned from a lengthy Pacific cruise aboard the USS Boxer, and Chuck was an experienced F8F fighter pilot.

Soon after the "Blues" arrived, Johnny Magda asked his F8F pilots who felt they were ready to fly the Panther to hold up their hands. Chuck O'Reilly did so and then got with Jake Robcke to show him how to start the Panther. Jake obliged with a cockpit checkout and also included a few additional tips, hoping that more information might prevent a gung-ho ensign named O'Reilly from killing himself on his first jet flight.

Chuck got the F9 into the air, careful to hold his right elbow into his gut so as not to over-control, then began his climb to 25,000 feet. He headed for the area of Hamilton Air Force Base northeast of the San Francisco Bay Area. Hamilton was where several Air Force jet squadrons were stationed.

Chuck says that he was only getting out of the crowded area.

He had not been in the air fifteen minutes, still looking around the cockpit between scans for other aircraft, and asking himself "What did Jake say this was for?" when he was joined on by an Air Force F-84 Thunderjet. The 84 pilot pulled alongside and signaled to Chuck, "Let's dogfight." Chuck paused for a second, decided "Why not," then signaled back an enthusiastic "OK." The Air Force pilot gave a nod and broke away to the north. Chuck started to turn south, then decided that turning away from the F-84 was not his smartest move. He figured he had best keep the other guy in sight and not have to search the skies for a hard-to-see jet fighter. This would also allow Chuck the opportunity to glance inside the cockpit in case he needed to find the right button to push. So Chuck turned north also. Then he moved his throttle to 100-percent power and pushed over to gain all the speed he could before the F-84 began to turn back. By then, Chuck was below the Thunderjet and indicating over 400 knots. When the F-84 pilot completed his turn back to the south and began his search for Chuck's Navy F9, it was nowhere in sight.

O'Reilly had used his tremendous speed and full power to climb quickly as the F-84 made his turn. He simply dropped behind the Air Force jet into perfect position for a kill. Chuck trailed the Thunderjet for a moment, then the F-84 gave the signal for a join-up. Chuck was still moving fast, not sure he could control the Panther well enough to join safely, so he pulled ahead and gave the Thunderjet the signal to join on him.

When the F-84 was comfortably joined on Chuck's wing, the Air Force pilot flashed a half smile, followed by a push-away sign with his hand, indicating "You're too good for me," then broke sharply away and headed for home.

Chuck says he won that fight solely by intimidation. "When that Thunderjet jock joined on me and saw my shiny Blue Angel paint job, he was dead meat."

Chapter 16

Ken Wallace was flying the old straight wing Panther jet in VF-191 when I was flying ADs in VA-195. We both made our first combat flights during December of 1950, flying from the deck of the USS Princeton. These days, Ken and I sometimes meet at the Naval Aviation Museum in Pensacola for lunch.

During one of our recent meetings, Ken mentioned the time Frank Soberski had trouble during jet carrier qualifications, when Air Group Nineteen was getting ready to embark for Korea. I remembered Frank well. We called him Sober, and I have always thought of him as one of the best and luckiest pilots I have ever known. Frank and I had just returned from a long Pacific cruise aboard the USS Boxer when the Korean War began. On the Boxer cruise, Frank was in VF-191, flying propeller-driven F8F Bearcats.

I recalled the day Sober was flat on his back in a Bearcat right alongside the Boxer. His F8F had caught turbulence just before landing and instantly flipped onto its back. A photographer aboard snapped a spectacular shot, which was later published in Life magazine. Just after the click of the camera, Frank calmly lowered the nose of his F8, rolled to an upright position, and came around for another pass and smooth landing. Those of us observing from "vulture's row," high above the flight deck, gave Soberski a nice round of applause as he casually climbed from the Bearcat and walked across the windy flight deck. Frank looked up, grinned, and gave a nice theatrical bow.

But the incident involving Frank Soberski that Ken Wallace spoke of was much more serious. Ken and Sober were both flying F9F straight-wing Panthers from the deck of the Princeton during carrier qualifications off San Francisco. Ken was on the starboard cat and had received the catapult officer's signal for a full power turn-up, just as Frank Soberski was over the ramp of the carrier and received a cut for landing. A VF-191 Panther being used that day by a photo pilot was behind Ken, waiting to pull onto the starboard catapult as soon as Ken was launched. Behind the photo pilot's plane was Scotty Jones in another F9, also waiting his turn.

Sober cut power and his jet touched down in good position to catch number three wire. But the F9's hook bounced and stayed in the up position too long, because the hold-down tension on the tail hook was not working properly. The hook continued to bounce and stay up all the way past number nine wire, Sober's last chance for an arrested landing before hitting the barricade. At high speed, Frank Soberski's F9F went through the barrier of steel and nylon straps that stretched across the Princeton's flight deck. The barricade installed was one designed for the F7F, a higher twin-engine propeller aircraft; it had little effect on the low, slick Panther.

Ken Wallace had applied full power to his jet engine, checked all of his cockpit gauges and was ready for a cat shot. He turned to his right to receive the launch signal from the catapult officer. Ken said there was not a soul in sight. Everyone forward on the flight deck had disappeared into the catwalks. Ken kept full power on his F9 for a long moment, because he was afraid the catapult might still fire; then he cut power when he became aware of an aircraft sliding toward him.

Frank Soberski's Panther struck the two F9Fs waiting to launch behind Ken Wallace. Scotty Jones' F9 wound up without a tail section, then Sober's Panther bounced off the photo plane leaving his starboard wing on the flight deck. Soberski, still strapped into the cockpit of what was left of his aircraft, continued sliding up the flight deck towards the launching catapult. The nose of Soberski's jet came within feet of Ken's cockpit, but the two aircraft never touched. Soberski's F9 wound up hanging on the round down at the bow of the carrier, with Frank staring into green water. No one was seriously injured and this ended Frank Soberski's second lucky break.

Frank's third escape from death was the most frightening of all. It came months later. Frank and Pat Murphy were flying F9Fs on a low-level mission near Wonsan Harbor, when several 50-caliber bullets struck Soberski's Panther. One of the shells penetrated Sober's windshield and fragments from the explosion shattered into Frank's face and blinded him. Pat Murphy quickly joined on Frank's wing and gave constant instructions so that Sober could keep his F9 under control. The flight was too far north to consider making it to a friendly landing strip, thus, landing back aboard the carrier blind and bleeding, ditching in freezing ocean water, or ejecting for a parachute drop into those same cold waters were Frank's only choices.

Pat Murphy was an experienced Blue Angel jet pilot, who had joined VF-191 with the rest of the Blue's team shortly after the beginning of the Korean War. Pat assured Sober that he could guide him to a safe landing aboard the carrier. Frank says that while he was sitting bloody and blinded in the cockpit of an F9F listening to Murphy's verbal reassurances, he was remembering an old joke about a Chicago attorney pleading with his client in a soft reassuring voice, saying "Trust Me!" But Frank pushed the thought aside. He had little choice but to have faith that Pat Murphy and the Landing Signal Officer aboard the Princeton would guide him to a safe landing.

The LSO waiting on the Princeton that day was Mabry Blaylock. When he received word that a jet was coming in with a blinded pilot, he called another LSO, George Parker, for assistance. He told George that the mike at the fantail was not working properly and that he would like to have both a mike and paddles to work the jet aboard.

George dashed to the office of the Air Boss high in the island structure of the Princeton. From there he had a good view of the entire operation and could communicate with both the pilot and with Mabry Blaylock. He told Mabry to drop the screen behind the LSO platform so he could see the signals of the paddles. George then proceeded to give voice instructions that could be heard by both Frank Soberski and Mabry Blaylock. Mabry then gave paddle signals to reinforce the communication.

George Parker still remembers well the day Soberski landed blind. He says that he appreciates the credit that has been given him through the years, but that the truth of the matter is that Pat Murphy flew Soberski to the ramp of the carrier in such good shape that about all the LSO had to do was signal a cut.

Frank Soberski, Pat Murphy, and the LSOs accomplished an amazing feat that day. The entire episode has been featured in a major motion picture titled *Men of the Fighting Lady*, and the photograph of Frank, with blood covering the front of his face and flight suit as he was assisted from his aircraft, has been published by *Life* magazine and others.

During our lunch at the museum, Ken and I recalled Frank's blind landing, and both of us had difficulty trying to imagine the sensation of landing aboard a carrier without eyesight. A pilot flies his aircraft by converting visual perception into proper movement of controls. When outside visibility is nonexistent, the pilot relies on instruments in the cockpit, but without vision and relying totally on voice instruction to make the necessary control movements to land a jet aboard a straight-deck carrier is a feat difficult to comprehend. When you add the anxiety of injuries and not knowing how serious they might be, then the imagining becomes even more complex.

Fifty-plus years can bring forth many changes in the

world in which we live. Today, if you are an opera fan in the Chicago area, particularly around the suburb of Willmette, you might know the name Frank Soberski. Not as a highly skilled jet pioneer and a very lucky fellow, nor as a famous opera performer, but as a quiet and non-assuming elderly gentleman who has served as president and committee chairman of various groups supporting opera in the Windy City for many years. Navy pilots are not commonly known for their involvement with the opera community, but Frank Soberski has never been one to fit comfortably into a preconceived mold.

Frank recovered from his injuries and flew in the Navy for over twenty years before retiring to start a professional engineering firm in Chicago. Today, Frank says that he much prefers to relax and listen to the Lyric Opera Company of Chicago perform *La Traviata* than to the voice of Pat Murphy speaking into his earphones saying, "Trust Me!" But when asked if he ever thinks now and then about earlier times, that old patented Soberski grin reruns, and along with the grin there appears a singular glow that can only be seen on occasion in the eyes of a few exceptional men.

I do enjoy my lunches with Ken Wallace.

The day was scheduled to be special. The word had been out for some time. During the past week smiles had grown from faint to immense. Laughter and slaps on the back were becoming routine.

Finally the rumors became official. Late the day before,

word had been passed that in 24 hours the USS Princeton would steam for Japan, and from there Air Group Nineteen was headed home.

Our Tiger Division was scheduled for the afternoon of our last day of combat. After takeoff the join up with other aircraft was precise. Heads were turning in cockpits to make certain that all was clear. No rushing to complete a fast rendezvous. No wings thrown up to slow the aircraft at the last moment — nothing that would risk a last-mission mid-air collision.

There was only brief, explicit radio chatter. Targets were hit quickly and cleanly with little comment. Those locations that contained heavy concentrations of enemy anti-aircraft fire were given a wide berth.

During the return flight to the carrier, every pilot listened carefully to make certain that his engine was purring like a kitten. Fuel remaining was given thoughtful attention. Oil pressure and temperature readings were monitored with every scan of the instruments. Nearly every landing was a roger pass all the way — number three wire, then a long burst of power to get forward as quickly as possible. On this last and very special day, no one wanted to take a chance on being chopped by a propeller from the plane behind.

As soon as the chocks were in place, switches were secured. Propellers made their final turns. The swishing sound of moving pistons turned to silence. As we hurried below for a quick debrief, our plane captain's congenial slap on the back still lingered between shoulder blades.

For the last time we looked up to study the island structure that towered alongside the flight deck. We searched for familiar faces that might be staring down from "vultures row." As we made our way across the worn and rocking teakwood deck, each of us carrying a plotting board and bag of maps, we leaned against a stiff wind that rushed across the flight deck. We breathed deeply of the cold open sea air. As the carrier commenced its turn out of the wind, the scent of stack gases added a distinctive odor.

Everyone in the Air Group was suffering from an acute case of short-timer's syndrome. This included intelligence-types who today asked only quick and precise questions. Answers were given in the same manner. There was little banter — no long-winded discussion of useless details. The job was soon completed.

Then it was time to unwind. Concerned faces began their slow transition towards relaxation. A few smiles broke through. The business of war and targets and airplanes and pilots who had not made it back to the carrier was put aside. The debriefing officers filed their reports and pilots departed for their ready rooms.

Dave, Jake, 'Pointer and myself — Dave Davidson's Tiger Division — headed for our dive-bomber's sanctuary, ready room four. After struggling our way out of miserable rubber survival suits, we slipped into comfortable khaki as quickly as we could.

Before we were settled into our seats the booze appeared. First the flight surgeons arrived with boxes of medicinal brandy packaged in small bottles. Then, as if by magic, fifths of bourbon, scotch, and gin materialized from nooks, crannies, and room safes. Hearty laughter, raised voices, and shouts of, "Mama, your lover is comin' home!" began to resonate around the ready room.

Only a few organized and thinking types made it to the wardroom for dinner. Most of us just sat. We talked and we drank. We laughed and we told jokes. Very much like we were back in school and had just completed exam week. Going home alive was beginning to settle into our being.

Many months before, the Princeton had steamed at near full speed, taking us from Hawaii to Korea in early December. In November hundreds of thousands of Chinese had suddenly appeared from nowhere in the snow-covered mountains and valleys of North Korea. Thousands of our Marine and Army troops were caught in traps all across Korea. Our job was close air support — napalm, bomb, and machine-gun the enemy until a path was cleared that allowed our guys to fight their way out.

Then began months of knocking out bridges, tunnels, trains and convoys, trying to stop the flow of supplies and troops from China to North Korea. Our efforts had cost the lives of 12 of our pilots, and now, on May 17, 1951, we were headed for home.

The talking and drinking continued until late in the evening. It was after midnight when someone came up with the brilliant idea of throwing all our maps and charts into the cold waters of the Sea of Japan.

Of all the many suggestions made that night, this one seemed to grab our group where we lived. Such creative thought! A genius of an idea! Now we had something that would allow us to take physical action. There were immediate whoops of joy. What could be more fitting than leaving symbols of our miserable, rubber-suited war buried beneath a sea of cold waters that for centuries had embraced the remains of forgotten warriors?

Many of us began to dash about, collecting our personal stashes of handmade maps. They covered all of North Korea, and each of us had spent hours cutting and shaping large charts into small sections. We covered them with clear plastic so that they could be easily stored. This prevented us from having navigational charts spread all over the cockpit while we tried to fly formation and keep track of where we were at the same time. A Navy pilot in Korea never knew when he would suddenly find himself on his own, flying over snow-covered mountains that looked the same, 50-knot winds that constantly tried to blow him off course, no radio beams to follow, and a carrier to find that was somewhere far out at sea.

From plotting boards and lockers the maps came. Stacks and stacks were placed into bags that could be carried to the catwalk, a small walkway where the square sheets of plastic could be thrown into the rushing sea below. When we opened the hatch that led to the nearest catwalk, the hard cold wind nearly sobered us enough to clear our minds and restore logical thinking. But booze won the night. Despite the near-hurricane-force gale that roared around the narrow walkway, we were able to bury our war.

"Goodbye Frozen Chosin," someone bellowed, whirling a chart marked with grease pencil hard into the tempest. Then it was a continuing series of shouts: "Goodbye Hwachon Reservoir," "Goodbye Sinpo," "Goodbye K-18." Each of us joined in the shouts, and soon we were having more fun than during our best snowball fight ever.

Throwing our memories of the last few months into the cold waters below released a ton of tension and anxiety. Having to fight roaring, frigid, swirling winds made the task even more pleasurable.

After the bags were empty and we had left the freezing cold of the catwalk for the warmth of the ready room, we quickly realized that the group had run out of gas. Suddenly the thought of bed had great appeal.

The next thing I remember is being shaken awake by the duty officer's messenger and sluggishly realizing that the pounding, rumbling, and whistling sound of our catapults launching aircraft was not a dream, but real.

"Wake up sir. You are flying in one hour!"

I opened one eye and stared. The kid was not joking. He was still holding my shoulders tightly. His eyes glared with that ponderous concern of youth as he tried to get some kind of acknowledgement that I was awake.

And suddenly I was. The rush of a massive hangover hit my head and my stomach at the same instant. The messenger helped me to my feet.

"Are you OK, sir?"

What a stupid question. But before I said what I wanted to say, old training surfaced and I managed a faint smile. I mumbled something halfway polite and then began a stumbling amble towards the head and shower. It took three tries at turning the water faucets before I realized that water hours were still in effect. No shower. Everything was coming up roses. Just absolutely and beautifully go-to-hell fantastic.

By the time I made it to ready four, Dave and Jake and 'Pointer were already halfway into their survival suits. As I began to get into my own outfit, the rubber felt harder and stiffer and more miserable than ever before.

It was a little after seven and we were scheduled to launch at eight. I soon learned that Commander Dick Merrick, our Air Group Commander, had launched his flight near dawn. The Chinese and North Koreans had begun a massive attack, and the USS Princeton was ordered back to the line to give emergency close air support to our Army and Marine troops being overrun by the thousands.

During our briefing for the flight, we learned that the new offensive was indeed enormous. We also learned that Commander Merrick and one of our other pilots were already dead. Shot down. No chutes. No chance of survival.

Luckily, Dave Davidson had held onto a few of his charts. "To go with my memoirs," he had said.

We made it to our aircraft, started engines on command, and as I pulled up alongside the Flight Deck Officer and added full power for takeoff, my thoughts were, "Here goes nothing. Just drop the damn flag."

And he did. I released the brakes, and for the first and only time in my life I flew an airplane into the air while still drunk. It was one of those wretched mornings with a high, gray overcast but no horizon. The cloud cover blended into the sea. Dave was still in his turn to allow us a fast rendezvous, and, as I came up to join on his wing, a touch of vertigo hit me. For a moment I thought I was going to lose it.

"What in the hell am I doing here?" I remember the feeling as though it were yesterday and vowed then and there, "Never again!"

About the time I finally settled into my number-two spot, it dawned on me to check Jake and 'Pointer. They were probably in as bad a shape as I was. But some of us are smarter than others. Jake and 'Pointer made no attempt to join in close formation. They just trailed well behind and slowly pulled into position while we headed for our target.

Someone in the ready room had pushed a can of tomato juice and a small thermos of coffee into the leg pockets on my flight suit. When we were pretty much squared away, headed to knock out a bridge at Chowon, I remembered the juice and coffee. It saved the day, and pretty soon Dave called, "Tiger One, rolling in!"

It is amazing how the human body can sometimes function with near perfection despite stupid and irresponsible treatment. Tiger Flight bombed as well that day as at any time I can remember. We each made two runs, and the bridge at Chowon was on the ground.

The next day we flew close air support for some of our guys who were fighting viciously to prevent entrapment near Changhyon-ni. When we returned to the ship, we learned that we were headed for home, again.

That night most of us watched a movie on the hanger

deck. I do not remember a single person even suggesting a celebration.

The Princeton unloaded our Air Group personnel in Japan and we were flown back to California via Hawaii. Air Group Nineteen aircraft remained aboard the Princeton and were transferred to a Reserve Group recalled for Korea.

When we got to Hawaii, several of us ordered leis to be sent to our wives. We somehow reasoned that this would help make up for our being two days late.

Deep within us, the silent part of our brain calculated that once the committee working on the cruise book had changed the number of pilots lost from 12 to 14, then again, all would be right with the world.

Chapter 17

Some of life's happenings are harder to put into words than others. It is often difficult to understand why. Since I began this book, I have known that I would try to write about Hap Harris, and I have started to do so on many occasions. Each time, I set my attempts aside. I thought I would have plenty of time. I would do it later. As time passed, I reflected more and more on why writing about Hap felt different than writing of many others who died while flying from carriers in Korea.

My youngest son, Greg, is a very good writer. Recently, in one of his notes to me he stated, "As a writer I always say, 'It's hard to get at the truth if you're forced to stick to the facts.'" I do not know if this is a "Greg original," but it certainly hit home with me.

After reading his note, I reread parts of Greg's last book. In particular I studied his chapter concerning the death of one of his brothers. He was Annie's and my number two son, Flip. Again the tears came, and the old hurt like no other hurt, and I thought how difficult this must have been for Greg. And then truth began to find its way to the surface. It occurred to me why I have a stronger urge at this time to write of Hap Harris, who died more than 50 years ago, than I do to write of my own son who has been gone only three years.

When Flip died, I wrote his obituary. It was not a standard for such writing. I said what I wanted to say, the paper printed it like I wrote it, and that ended it for me for a while. Then my son Greg wrote beautifully of Flip in his book. My oldest son, Tiger, created a web page, and the rest of the family has preserved Flip's memory in thought and deed to the extent that I am comfortable that Flip will be remembered in the special way that he was special.

Most of the above is true of Hap Harris, but it is not enough for me. I remember a Hap that I have never seen in writing nor heard discussed by others. It is the same when I recall many parts of the Korean War. To me, the death of Hap Harris symbolizes the tragedy of that war, as did the death of a pilot named Brubaker, who became the focus for Michener in his book, *The Bridges at Toko Ri*.

However, a major difference sticks in my mind. Brubaker is a fictitious character. Hap Harris lived and breathed, and laughed and joked, and played a ukulele and sang, and loved with all his heart a real live beautiful girl named Ann. And Ann became his wife and loved him back with an intensity that somehow can only be captured by the young. And the two of them dreamed, and tingled with excitement while planning for the future, the same as you and I and a multitude of others. But for Ann and Hap it all ceased with the abruptness and rudeness of sudden death. Seven months after their exchanging "I do's," Hap's aircraft was hit by a solid burst of anti-aircraft fire and within seconds crashed into freezing waters off the coast of North Korea.

When I reported aboard my first fleet squadron, VA-195, in the fall of 1949, there were only three people I recognized immediately. One was Don Van Slooten, my old classmate from preflight. The second was Don Munday, who had dated my future sister-in-law, Sabra (Annie's sister), during our training in Pensacola. The third was Hap Harris. I wrote earlier of Hap and the South American pilot who flew Hap under bridges and then asked, "You don' wan' to die?" We all remember those who can tell a story and make us laugh, and I immediately remembered Hap and our group who bummed airplane rides on weekends while going through preflight.

Hap probably did not remember me at that time, since I had been a few months behind him in training. He was already established in the squadron, and I was just another pilot reporting aboard. But he was friendly and remembered the South American pilot story when I reminded him. For quite a long time our relationship was little different than that which each of us shared with other pilots in the squadron. We spent considerable time together aboard the USS Boxer during a peacetime cruise just before the Korean War started. We began to know one another well, but it was not until after we returned and married, and our wives became very good friends, that Hap and I became real buddies.

VA-195 pilots were close because there were only about 20 or so of us, and we flew together and drank and partied together. On rainy days we played acey-deucey and bridge, and on Friday nights we all went to happy hour at the Officers' Club. There we relived the week. We talked about flying, about world happenings, guessed about our future, kidded the ones who were married and had to leave early, drank our beer, sang pilot songs, and in between we planned for the weekend. On Sundays we slowed down, and on Mondays we were bright-eyed and bushy-tailed, ready to fly.

The late 1940s were a peaceful interlude for our country. To a large extent our nation was just quietly catching its breath after World War II. Most of us thought of ourselves as part of the strongest power on earth — a country of righteous, virtuous, and noble citizens. The majority of our leaders were perceived to be honest, hard working and capable, and many of us aspired to walk in their footsteps. Responsible media did not print or speak of scandal until facts were proven.

I cannot recall a single pilot in our squadron who was not there because he very much wanted to be. When we went to a bar in uniform, strangers would oftentimes offer to buy us a drink. These offers were nearly always from men who remembered the price paid by our soldiers during the war. Most single women were shy and ladylike, reluctant to appear overly aggressive with strange men. But they often smiled.

There were events to come that would bring change. Perhaps the Korean War was the landmark for the beginning of that change, but in 1949 the great majority of our country remained a society of trust. There are those today, of course, who say we were naïve, and perhaps there is an element of truth in their allegation. Knowing my own thoughts and those of many with whom I have lived a lifetime, perhaps being a little naïve was not all that bad.

That is about the way our world was in December 1949, when Air Group Nineteen was ordered to prepare for an extended Western Pacific cruise aboard the USS Boxer. Our mission was to visit the major ports of Asia, while perfecting our abilities to operate our aircraft from a carrier. I do not know if our present Navy still uses the term, "flag-waving cruise," but the words clearly describe what our tour aboard the Boxer was to be.

The first order of business for VA-195 was to get all of our pilots carrier-qualified in the AD. This we did. Flying the AD aboard the carrier was enjoyable. She was a good stable aircraft with no surprises. We had no way of knowing then, but we were embarking on six months of rigorous fleet training, which would prepare us for a very tough war that would begin shortly after we returned.

Early in January 1950, we sailed beneath the Golden Gate Bridge and headed for Hawaii. During the next five months we waved the flag in Korea, Japan, Hong Kong, Manila, Singapore, and the Philippines. Hap and I lived in a large bunkroom called "Boy's Town," with several other junior ensigns. It was here that I first heard Hap sing and play the ukulele. He and three or four others entertained us regularly with stringed instruments. The tunes were all familiar, but we changed the words a bit. The songs we sang were mostly of flying and dying, drinking, and wild women. Some we wrote, some we inherited from World War I and World War II, and some probably went back to the days of the Wright brothers. None we composed were intended for polite company.

Then, on a very cold day in January 1950, the USS Boxer dropped anchor in Inchon Harbor for a visit to Seoul, South Korea. Our Admiral visited President Rhee at his palace, and Boxer officers were invited to a reception following the official exchange of diplomatic talk. The meeting hall was so cold that we junior officers kept our heavy black topcoats on and formed a group close to the bar, trying to stay warm. Here we were greeted by a friendly Catholic bishop. I have always wished that I had made a note to remember his name but, sadly, I did not. He proved to be a very knowledgeable and discerning prophet.

The bishop told us a little of what was going on in North Korea. Hard-line communism was in full swing with the usual quick trial and often grim executions of nonbelievers. I will never forget his parting words to us: "This is not goodbye. Many of you will be back here in a very short time." How right he was.

We returned to the States in mid June. Throughout the cruise most of the talk among us ensigns who had been Flying Midshipmen had to do with our impending departure from the Navy. Our contract called for discharge if not selected for Regular Navy within a short time after commission. Harry Truman was President. His ax-man was Secretary of Defense Johnson. The war was over. Our country wanted a small military. In our group of nearly 200 new ensigns, highly qualified as fleet carrier pilots, only three were selected to remain in the Regular Navy. The rest of us were scheduled for discharge with the option of serving in the reserves. We did have two years of college coming to us from our contract and, in addition, the GI Bill. So we were not exactly being tossed to the wolves. However, nearly all of us — to the man — wanted to remain in the Navy and fly airplanes.

Hap and I and several others had made plans to enroll at the University of Colorado. We envisioned skiing in beautiful mountains and drinking hot buttered rums with pretty young snow bunnies. Perhaps there was some thought given to books and study. We did plan to marry one day, but, without our Navy officers' pay, there was simply not enough money for marriage until we earned a college degree.

The Navy has an old saying that has remained implanted in my mind since the day Executive Officer Dave Davidson added it to our list of one-liners concerning acquired wisdom: "If you cannot be good, make damn sure that you are lucky."

On June 25, 1950, I was one of about 200 ensigns at the Navy Base at Treasure Island near San Francisco who were scheduled to be thrown out of the Navy by June 30. When the Korean War suddenly broke out that very day, well, I hesitate to say so, but the honest-to-god truth is that many of us felt lucky. No sooner do I write such words than my son Greg's remark that truth can be difficult enters my mind, and tagging alongside is an even stronger sense of guilt.

Over 40,000 of our servicemen and women died in the Korean War. That is a heavy price to pay just to please a few young men who wanted to stay in the Navy and fly. But, at the time, we were shouting with excitement. Many of us were on the telephone trying to stop the civil service people at Treasure Island in their rush to get us out of the Navy. We quickly discovered that phone calls from ensigns to senior naval officers do not receive top priority. Despite our muddling, someone somewhere did something right and we were rushed back to our squadrons.

We all charged back to the Air Group, experienced salts with a carrier cruise under our belt. We were prepared to do bodily harm to any new ensigns who thought they could take our place.

Hap and I and others quickly blended back into squadron routine. During the coming weeks we filled old slots, and the best of the new arrivals were added to our roster. VA-195 was manned for war.

A couple of months later we were at NAS El Centro, California, undergoing intensive training for combat in Korea. Dave Davidson, our executive officer and division leader, was leading four of us back for landing when we heard the click of a transmitter. Then, a soft, hesitant voice: "Oops!" It was the same expression that a person might make who had just dropped a package, or bumped into someone accidentally; or, in the case of Hap Evan Harris, when he ran his AD out of gas!

Our division was in landing formation over the duty runway. Dave had just moved us into right echelon and was looking my way, ready to toss a casual salute and break for landing. Then Hap's plane, number four in the formation, dropped suddenly from the flight. Hap's section leader, Jake Jacobson, followed Hap. Dave Davidson, guessing what had happened, continued straight ahead to give Hap plenty of room to plan his landing. Hap called the tower and told them of his emergency. Silently,

Jake followed Hap, carefully checking that everything looked OK.

Hap landed the Skyraider dead stick in the first half of El Centro's duty runway. Doing this in a heavy fighter-bomber, suddenly without power, required great flying skill. To add a touch of class, Hap used his rollout speed to coast the AD clear of the duty runway — showmanship!

Later, at our favorite Westmoreland watering hole, Dave, Jake, and I thanked Hap most formally for clearing the duty runway quickly. Thoughtfulness from a fellow airplane driver is always appreciated. We then proceeded to stick Hap with the check. Running out of gas in an aircraft is always a drink-buying offense, even in the midst of preparation for war. While at El Centro, trying to get the most training in the time available, the squadron routinely switched pilots with the engines running. Overlooking normal routine, such as checking gas tanks, was an easy mistake to make.

Near the end of our two weeks in El Centro, Hap's new bride, Ann, and my own, Annie, traveled to Coronado, near San Diego, so that the four of us could have extra time together as guests of Ann's parents. When VA-195's Skyraiders launched for the cool of northern California, Hap and I boarded a Greyhound bus in 110-degree heat for the trip from El Centro to San Diego. There was no air conditioning. No fans. No cold beer. We sweated all the way to San Diego. Then, while Hap and I inhaled cool ones in Coronado, the girls told us all about their trip down. They had driven US 1 from San Francisco to San Diego — two days on dangerous mountain roads, each taking her turn to scream, because someone had convinced them that the scenery was worth the extra time.

Despite all, the trip turned out great. Ann's parents (who were also Navy) gave a party, and several local friends of Ann and Hap came. Hap and Ann played their ukes, we sang old songs, and Ann taught the girls how to do Hawaiian dances.

The next day the four of us packed the car and headed for Alameda. We drove most of the day, and in the wee hours of the morning we stopped at a small motel. For some unknown reason Hap and I dreamed up a brilliant idea: We hid the girls in the car, paid for two rooms, then sneaked our brides up the back stairs. If the girls thought we were crazy, they didn't say so. They giggled all the way up the stairs.

In September we were back in Alameda, flying night and day to get ready for Korea. A three-day weekend came along, and Hap, Ann, Annie and I joined Don and Dee Munday (also newlyweds) for a camping trip on the Russian River north of San Francisco. Among us we managed to locate six sleeping bags and two tents. The first night we cut cards to see which couple got the privacy tent. Then we rotated.

It was cold from midnight on. At daylight a three-foot fog hung over the river. On the second morning Hap spotted "ducks." They were on our side of the river. Moving quietly so as not to wake the girls, Hap and I sneaked into our tent for shotguns. We were determined to have duck for breakfast.

Carefully, we crawled through thick, thorny underbrush, trying not to make a sound that would flush the ducks. It took half an hour to reach a good position from which we could make a decent shot. Finally we were ready. Hap signaled his target and I picked mine. We fired. The quiet of a perfect and very peaceful early morning was shattered by the two loud blasts. Two very ordinary and ugly California mud hens had been transported to looked-like-a-duck heaven.

After the excitement, Don Munday (the experienced Joplin, Missouri, hunter) had hot coffee, bacon and scrambled eggs ready. The three of us were joined by our now wide-awake brides. Don said he "knew all along that we would not have duck for breakfast." He just did not want to "spoil our fun." Looking back, I don't think anyone could have.

The USS Princeton, with our Air Group Nineteen aboard, left Alameda in November 1950. Annie and I waved until each of us could not see the other. Ann lost sight of Hap while the ship was still close. She told Annie later that she knew at that moment that she would never see Hap again. She knew there would be no more camping trips on the Russian river, no more rendezvous in Coronado. No more blending of two ukes to create a sound that only she and Hap could produce. No more crazy sneaking up back stairs to a motel room. Ann Harris also knew that she was pregnant.

On the way to Korea the Princeton stopped in Hawaii. We sailed in and out of the area for two weeks so that Air Group Nineteen could obtain additional training. Our aircraft were loaded to capacity with napalm, rocket, and various bomb loads. The feel of the AD when launched from a carrier deck at maximum weight was something new and required attention, but after a few flights that, too, became routine.

Those of us in VA-195 were very lucky. We were assigned an aircraft with only one engine, which could be launched from a carrier with a slightly larger bomb load than was carried by the four-engine B17 Flying Fortress of World War II. Instead of 10 crewmen and nearly that many guns, we had maneuverability, a powerful engine, and five years of extensive development that gave us many hours of staying time over the target.

The AD had been designed for World War II as a torpe-do and dive-bomber combination, but it was too late for the war. Thus, the engineers had many years to add improvements, which made the AD the best propeller-driven, close-air-support aircraft ever built. As historians are now recording, Korea was a Close Air Support War. Not an Air-to-Air War. For every hour of air-to-air combat in Korea, there were a thousand hours of close air support, where the lives of our troops on the ground hung on a pilot's ability to destroy enemy troops just a short distance away.

Off duty in Hawaii, we relaxed under a huge Banyan tree in the courtyard of the Moana Hotel on Waikiki beach. The Moana is next to the Royal Hawaiian. Many know the Royal Hawaiian. Navy pilots know the Moana. During the time of the Korean War, the Moana was cheaper. It also enjoyed a more relaxed and informal atmosphere.

During the time our Air Group was working and relaxing in Hawaii, Chinese soldiers were moving by night into northeast Korea. By late November nearly 20,000 US Marine and Army troops were trapped near the Chosin reservoir. The only way out was down a single narrow mountain road. The Chinese were dug into the high ground. The only hope for our guys was that abundant and effective close air support could be made available as quickly as possible.

Suddenly, our stay in Hawaii was ended. The Princeton left Hawaii and steamed for Korea. We came close to becoming another "31-Knot Burke," referring to a destroyer skipper in World War II who became a legend for speeding to intercept the enemy.

We reached the waters near Hungnam, Korea, 75 miles from the Chosin reservoir, on December 5. From that date until Christmas Eve, unless grounded by weather, we flew constant close air support to cover Marine and Army units. Air controllers on the ground and in the air marked the targets for our aircraft to strike.

Marine and Army units slowly and successfully, but with heavy losses, fought their way down the narrow road from the Chosin to the coast. The evacuation was completed on Christmas Eve, 1950.

In early January 1951, the Squadron was given a few days of liberty at a rest camp in the mountains of western Japan. One evening several of us decided to go native for sukiyaki. Hap had discovered a restaurant hidden in the nearby hills, which could be reached by cab. The tavern, which consisted of a few small paper rooms, was cold. Each little cubical was heated only with small charcoal pots. The same pots also were used for cooking. We sat on the floor around a large low table, bundled in our topcoats. Each of us tried to scoot closer to the nearest charcoal burner. Japanese waitresses wearing heavy silk kimonos chattered constantly in singsong Japanese, while serving hot sake in small delicate cups.

Before long the chill eased, and Hap broke out his ukulele. We sang many of the old songs we had composed during the Boxer cruise. With the heat from the charcoal pots, the warm sake, and the close company of good companionship, the lyrics sounded better and better.

The young waitresses listened and smiled. They continued to move busily, chattering continuously, adding charcoal to the fire and pouring more ingredients into the simmering sukiyaki. A great smell of deliciously seasoned food began to fill the small room. The sake was exerting its effect, and all the while the sliding paper walls and straw mats on the floor protected us from most of the cold mountain air.

The waitress who seemed to be in charge of the sukiyaki project opened a small woven basket and began removing eggs to break into the steaming pot. Hap caught her attention. He then took one of the eggs from her and placed it in his mouth. All the waitresses stopped and turned to stare with amazement. With facial expression and a little acting, Hap appeared to swallow the egg, shell and all. Then, with the smoothness of a good magician, Hap recovered the egg from beneath the pillow on which he sat. The girls shrieked with laughter. They continued to giggle, point at Hap, and chatter in Japanese.

Using broken English, they insisted that Hap repeat his trick.

When the last of the sukiyaki was gone (which was the best I have ever tasted), when all our songs had been sung, and after untold amounts of sake had been consumed, our small group huddled together for a freezing cab ride back to our hotel.

When we entered the lobby, I was surprised to learn that it was 3A.M.. Then we saw the bulletin board, outlining the next day's schedule of activities. Standing out in big print was "Pheasant Hunting With Guide and Dog," scheduled for 5A.M.. Guns and ammunition would be supplied. Without hesitation, Hap and I signed to be called at 4:30. The others had sobered enough to pass on it.

At sunrise, Hap and I, an aged and fragile Japanese guide who spoke not a word of English, and a small brown hunting dog were making our way along a narrow valley trail between beautiful snow-capped mountains. There was not a cloud in the deep blue sky. Small portions of the frigid air were transformed into little gray puffs of alcoholic smog as Hap and I trudged along, breathing hard, just trying to keep up.

Occasionally, our guide would stop and point into the brush ahead. Using a jumble of whispered, high-pitched, brisk Japanese, the small wrinkled and stooped man would instruct the dog: "That way. That way. Flush! Flush!"

The little brown dog would look hard at his frail master, give a little expression of comprehension, wag its tail, then disappear into the brush. A few minutes later we would hear the wonderful sound of pheasant wings flapping in the crisp morning air. The birds were always 30 yards behind us, flying swiftly in the opposite direction from where the guide had pointed. Hap and I had retained enough sake from the earlier hours to think the old guide and his little brown dog were about the funniest act around, but after an hour of hard walking and half a dozen wrong-direction flushes, we began to sober.

Then suddenly, not 20 yards ahead, three of the largest and most beautifully colored peasants I have ever seen were rising in front of me. By instinct I raised the shotgun and fired. There was no way to miss. There was a loud explosion and smoke — and I found myself holding only the stock of the shotgun. The barrel had blown completely off! I was stunned but not injured.

The Japanese guide now shouted excitedly, pointing first to me and then to the gun barrel, still smoking, lying on the ground. Hap was doubled over in laughter. The old dead-shot Texan had missed three pheasants from 20 yards.

We went back to sea in mid January. Hap was killed on January 28, 1951, during an attack on Sinpo, a hotbed of enemy activity and intense anti-aircraft fire near the Manchurian border on the East Coast of North Korea.

I will close this story with a letter from Don Van Slooten to my godson, Willie, Hap's son, which says a few things better than I would dare attempt.

Sunday, January 5, 1997

Dear Willie, Son of Hap,

It is my hope, after you have read these things that I will write to you, that you will have a better knowledge and understanding of your father's last flying mission and also an even deeper sense of what a noble and admirable title it is to be referred to as the "Son of Hap."

It is noteworthy that I write to you on a Sunday morning, because it was also on a Sunday morning in the late winter of 1951 that your father, whom we affectionately knew as "Hap," and Commander Swede Carlson and I, and, I believe, Darryl Skalla, were assigned to fly a special mission from the decks of the aircraft carrier Princeton, operating off the coast of North Korea.

Before relating the events of that mission, let me first share with you some of the things that we experienced, which might serve as a background for what happened on that fateful Sunday morning. It is also my desire to give you a little additional insight into the character of your father and also to make you aware of the great regard we all had for him.

I first came to know Hap when several of us who had recently completed advanced naval flight training in Corpus Christi, Texas, were preparing to join the Navy Attack Squadron, VA-195, in Alameda, California.

I was impressed, when I met Hap and began to associate with him, just how quickly he was liked and favorably regarded by his associates. I found him to be a very jovial, free-spirited man who loved life and enjoyed those around him. And, after flying with him, I also observed that he was a top-notch Navy pilot. We regarded him as one of the best.

I must tell you of an incident that happened some time before our Korea involvement. It relates directly to you, his then soon-to-be-born child.

With regard to Naval aviators, it can truly be said that they "live on the edge." One of the more difficult things that a carrier pilot must learn is the ability to fly slow, but not too slow. In a carrier landing approach, it is essential that the plane's speed be no more than a few knots above stalling speed so that when the Landing Signal Officer signals "cut the throttle," the pilot responds and the plane is then no longer flying but drops quickly to the carrier deck, catches a wire, and stays there. If there were excess speed, the plane would float or bounce into the planes parked toward the bow of the ship and that would result in all kinds of carnage.

Now, with that background, let me tell you how this relates to you. Prior to our departure for Korea, we were stationed at Naval Air Station, Alameda. There, of course, we had long runways on which to land. And, so, when landing there, we sneaked in a few extra knots to our approach speed because it just felt a little more safe and certainly more comfortable.

When Hap married Ann, we used to tease him, because it was obvious that he had added about five knots to his landing speed just to be a little safer for his new bride. It was also the topic of conversation around the squadron, after he announced that a child was on the way, that he added another five knots just for good measure. And so, you see, you influenced him for good, even before you arrived on the scene, and I hope this will also indicate to you the love your father had for you, even though your meeting one another hadn't occurred.

Now, to return to Korea. On that Sunday morning, it was still very cold, being in the late wintertime of the year. Ours was to be an early morning flight. We each put on the customary exposure suit, which was like stepping into a big rubber bag that formed to our legs, bodies, and arms, and was worn under our flight gear. We were told that wearing this would extend our ability to survive in the super cold ocean water for an additional several minutes if we should crash. So we tolerated the discomfort of wearing it.

The four of us mentioned had been given the mission to knock out a bridge that was part of a railway running along the coastline in the northern part of North Korea. In our ready room briefing prior to takeoff, we were made aware that our mission objective was considered to be of utmost importance. It had been observed that almost every night trains laden with ammunition and supplies were being sent by the Chinese to North Korean troops further down the peninsula, and these trains had to pass over the high and narrow railroad bridge that was to be our target objective that morning. It was further impressed upon us that a number of other pilots from the Air Force and from other Navy carriers had previously been sent to destroy this particular bridge but had been unsuccessful.

We took off from our USS Princeton flight deck in the first launch of the day. Three of us, including Hap, quickly joined up on the lead plane flown by Commander Carlson. We flew in a loose formation of four planes to the target area. The time it took to arrive there escapes me, but I speculate it would have probably taken about 30 minutes. I do remember that when we first spotted the targeted bridge, we also saw a surrounding landscape from about a mile on one side to a mile on the other that was pock-marked with holes from the many bombs that had previously been dropped during unsuccessful efforts of those trying to knock out this bridge, just as we were assigned to do on that morning.

Commander Carlson led our flight to the area and then set up a race track pattern with each of us flying about 20 seconds behind the plane in front of us. It became each of our turns to make a bombing run when we reached a point directly above the target. At that point, we would roll the plane over into a very steep, almost vertical, dive. Then we would "pop" the dive brakes, which were large panels that when hydraulically opened protruded from each side and the under side of the fuselage. These brakes prevented an excess buildup of speed, which would have prevented the maneuvering capability during the dive. We began each dive at an altitude of about 12,000 feet and came down so steep that we were no longer sitting in the seat but were hanging in our shoulder straps. Our purpose for being that steep was for the greater accuracy it gave us. After dropping the bomb for that run, we then pulled out of our dive at about 1,000 feet over the ground, proceeded to recover and climb in the race track pattern to the point of our next run.

Before we started these bombing runs, nestled under

the wing and fuselage of each of our planes were three 2,000-pound bombs. One bomb was dropped on each run. That meant that among the four of us we had 12 bombing passes to hit and destroy the bridge. But, after 11 such runs had been made, though we had some very near misses, the bridge was still standing with no serious damage incurred.

Only one of us had a bomb remaining. That was Hap. As the other three planes circled above, Hap rolled over and started into his final dive. From above, we watched with great hope and concern. Then one of us spotted the hit and called out, "He got it! A direct hit!! The bridge is gone!!!" We literally shouted over the radio, so pleased were we with the results at that moment. Hap had destroyed the bridge. What so many others had been unable to do, Hap had accomplished.

It was with a feeling of great jubilation that we then left the area and headed up the coast to what had been assigned as a secondary target. We had been informed in our pre-takeoff briefing that there were sheds or warehouses in a town up the coastline that probably had strategic enemy military supplies in them. When we got to the area, Commander Carlson had us break from the formation and each seek such targets, and, when we had located them, to destroy them using the planes' 20-millimeter cannons.

After approximately 15 minutes, with each of us making independent runs, usually from the direction of the sea toward the town, Commander Carlson's radio message came, giving us directions to rejoin our flight formation preparatory to flying back to the carrier. At that point, Hap identified himself on the radio and stated that he had located another target and requested permission to make one more run. The permission was granted and the others of us started our join-up.

We had no sooner started this when we heard the electrifying distress call on the radio, "Mayday, Mayday, Mayday!" Then all was silent. The suddenness and the surprise of this stunned each of us. At that point, the silence was broken as Commander Carlson called us one by one to determine from which plane the distress signal had come. Each of us responded as he was called, except Hap.

Then we looked down into the bay below and saw the sickening splash mark where a plane had crashed in the water. Commander Carlson descended to have a closer look. A dye marker, the kind attached to a pilot's life vest began to spread a large light green colored spot in the water where the plane had crashed. It was soon obvious that there was no chance that Hap had survived.

In the hopes that Hap's body might be recovered from the shallow bay, Commander Carlson radioed to others in the area for the kind of help that might accomplish that. We then continued to circle overhead to give protection to the hoped-for recovery effort. After a time, with our planes' fuel levels becoming low, we were forced to leave the area and return to the carrier. We learned later in the day, however, that other pilots came and continued to circle the area while efforts were made to recover Hap's body. Unfortunately, these efforts were not successful.

It became evident that this area, where we had been

flying, was an enemy-fortified hotspot. We learned by the end of that day, that in addition to Hap, two other pilots had been shot down and killed during the attempted recovery effort.

When we returned to the ship, as was customary, the pilots of the mission were debriefed and interrogated about the events of the previous three hours. I remember that I literally sobbed during this debriefing. It was tremendously hard to come to grips with the sudden death and departure of this good friend and flying comrade.

It is still hard to come to grips with events such as this. One asks, "Why? What was accomplished? Wasn't the price too high to pay?" As a father who has raised four sons, if I contemplate the thought of having been deprived of that privilege, or of having had my sons grow up without a father, I realize that the price Hap and his family paid is overwhelming. Probably none of us can really appreciate how great for them the price has really been.

It is reasonable to ask, "What was accomplished?" It is hard to know for a certainty what the results actually were. I wonder, however, if there are not men living today who did return home and who did raise sons, and families who might not have had that privilege had Hap not destroyed that bridge and interrupted the enemy supply line. I wonder if lives were not spared because the bullets that would have snuffed out these persons' lives did not reach the enemy's fighting troops and guns as a direct result of the very heroic actions and wonderful flying abilities of Hap Harris on that Sunday morning. It is my conjecture that it is entirely possible that this is so.

Be that as it may, I only know that I, for one, am deeply, deeply appreciative of the freedoms that I enjoy in this great country of ours. This is particularly true when I hear of others throughout the world who live in "police" states where freedoms are curtailed. Especially, when I hear of their living in such terrible and often fearful conditions, my appreciation to men like Hap Harris knows no bounds.

On that Sunday morning long ago in Korea, I became more intensely aware of the extreme price that some have paid for this wonderful freedom that we enjoy. Thank you, Willie, "Son of Hap." I will always be grateful.

With Great Appreciation,

Don Van Slooten
Friend and Flying Comrade of Hap

Afterword

The restoration of the Hill County Court House was complete, and on the last Saturday of April 1999 Willie Nelson and his band returned to lead the celebration. Six years had elapsed since a raging New Year's Day fire brought the old landmark to the ground. I had been determined to take my mother from Florida to Texas for the festivities, knowing it would be her last journey to Hillsboro. She had been determined to go, but her doctors advised strongly against the trip, and, in the end, she heeded their warnings. Annie and I traveled alone.

We stayed with old and good friends and blended with the huge crowds of Hill County natives while we toured the resurrected landmark. We gazed with wonderment and admired the exceptional workmanship. We reached and touched beautiful old wood and stone that had been salvaged — some say rescued — from aged and dying buildings all over Texas. Elderly craftsmen, using skills that are now mostly forgotten, had created a modern Phoenix. The magnificence of the new somehow surpasses memories of the old.

Before the concert, using the courthouse to provide a

towering backdrop of rugged Texas limestone that appeared golden in the afternoon sun, Governor George W. Bush spoke important words. He spoke about small towns and strong families, about communities pulling together to accomplish a common good. He spoke of how this country came to be encased in greatness and he gave all of us firm reminders of what is required to preserve that greatness.

As he talked, my mind wandered to memories of his father, our past president and a World War II Navy pilot. His father had spoken to a group of Navy pilots just a few years before in Pensacola. Both father and son used words that expressed the quiet and personal thoughts of many.

Then the newly risen courthouse clock struck the hour, and I recalled that Mama had told me about the re-builders getting old Hillsboro natives together to listen to bongs from the new bell to determine if the new sounds matched the old. Mama told me that there was a slight difference but that she could not put into words what the difference was. She was right. The exact sound of aged metal striking other aged metal is difficult to duplicate.

The same is true when attempting to recall human events and emotions. Memories replayed are never true replicas of the moments that gave them birth. But reflection, like good wine if handled with care, can age into something special.

The next day my friend drove me around Hillsboro to take a few photographs. After the last picture was snapped, day had turned to evening and the sun was only a red glow in the western sky. I gazed towards a horizon where cowboys once parked herds of cattle on their way to northern markets. They rode horseback into Hillsboro. They, too, breathed the fragrance of an evening air filled with smells of wildflowers and cattle, of cotton and corn and good living.

Then we drove by one of the spots where I had parked my Model-A more than 50 years before. I got out of the car and walked alone, gazing at a skyline where I could see again the lighted clock tower of the newly risen courthouse. I remembered a time in 1953 when I led a flight of seven French students over Hillsboro. We were flying World War II F6Fs, on our way to Oklahoma City from Corpus Christi to celebrate the students' graduation from advanced flight training. We circled low over Hillsboro because they had heard me brag so much about my hometown that they wanted to see for themselves. Not long after, most of those seven students were circling over a land then called French Indo-China. Some of them died there, and the only sense that can be made of their deaths is that they and many of their countrymen provided the overture for our own country's Vietnam.

While standing quietly in the small grass clearing where I had stood so many years before, I remembered a writing professor in college. He used a special technique for starting each of his classes. He would enter the classroom with a distinctive and confident flair. Then, using the methodology of Jack Benny, he would wait patiently until he had our undivided attention. When the moment was right, the professor would take a piece of chalk, and starting at the top left side of a blackboard that covered the entire front of the classroom, he would draw a line all the way to the lower right side of the board.

Making superb use of one final pause, the old professor would turn to face the class. Speaking with a firm and refined voice he would ask: "What does this mean?" And all of us in the classroom would answer loudly and in unison, "Every good story must have an angle!"

As I again studied the darkening horizon, knowing that I would try to put into words what I was feeling, I reminded myself of the professor's challenge. I thought anew about Scarsheim's last transmission and his screams: "I'm on Fire! I'm on Fire!" and remembered the silence that followed. I reminisced about Dave Davidson and all that he taught so many of us. And Swede Carlson and Marian the librarian. Again, I sensed the terror that gripped Harry White when he put that first torpedo into the solid wall of flashing death that was the Yamato. And I remembered the strange smile that was on Tom Dreis's face when he told us ensigns exactly what we wanted to hear following our Suhio Dam strike.

I recalled the whispered transmission of the ground controller when my bombs turned over a hundred yards of trenches that were packed tight with enemy soldiers into nothing but smoke and dust: "Good God Almighty!" And I thought of my friend Gus Hilton whose ashes now mingle with the stone of Hill County's newly risen courthouse. I remembered his words following my coward cure that night in the college dormitory: "Let's get some sleep, Old Buddy."

I could hear again the sobs of Don Van Slooten at the debriefing following Hap's death. It became clear to me that Van's sobbing summed up many things better than words. Words totally fail to express the grief that Van then knew must be relayed to Hap's wife, Ann, to his family, and later to his newborn son. Van was sobbing for all of us — for all those years of memories that had been Hap Harris, which would now remain for all time just that, memories.

Then I was ready with a mental answer for my old writing professor. I summoned forth vivid recollections of the aged black lady in New Orleans who grieved so intensely over the senseless death of her grandson. I perceived again her anguish and heartbreak, able to see only that minuscule part of the iceberg that lay quietly atop the enormous mass of pain hidden beneath. I remembered her simple reply to Rick Bragg when asked why she bothered to thank him for writing of her grandson's death: "You sees sir, if it ain't writ down, peoples forgits."

So I have written words. Hopefully, some of them will be words that will someday help others to know better the happenings and reflections of a few who shared a long-ago time and a nearly forgotten war.

In looking back, my mind is clear in knowing that it was not the happenings, it was the people. It is those moments of shared closeness and intense kinship with other human beings that dominate my memories. This of course is true in all lives, in all circumstances; but war — in addition to all that accompanies its presence — also serves to intensify and condense relationships. Those of us who flew from carriers in Korea, as well as other warriors from other wars, were often together for only a short time, yet we sometimes travel thousands of miles to spend just a few hours of intense and shared remembering.

Living is a combination of many things, perhaps too complex for the human mind. But some things we do know: The excitement of young love and the grace with which it ages. The birth of a child, the laughter of children. The magnificence of great art, a sunset, a sunrise, an ocean, a mountain. A really great book or movie, and of course our music, which captures all human emotions. The making of a new and true friend, and the death of those closest to us. With all of these happenings there comes a powerful compulsion to share our thoughts and our emotions with those who are most important in our lives.

Korea, as wars go, was not the largest, but fervor and emotion were there in spades. As the years since have gathered to form more than half a century, those of us who survived Korea have become old soldiers. And like many an old soldier who has gone before, our reminiscing has increased with each passing year. And we come to know again that it was the people — not just the happenings — that have become ingrained and are now an essential part of our being.

Thus, my attempt to "writ it down" must fall short, because words tell with clarity only the happenings. They can, when used with care, tell what old soldiers said and what they did, but never, with absolute precision, record what they feel and what they felt.

Acknowledgments

Most first-time book writers need all the help they can find. I know I did, and I was not bashful in asking old friends, and sometimes total strangers, to stop what they were doing and read my stories. As a whole, they were a tactful group. Some said they enjoyed the reading and then quickly began an extended talk about the weather. Some had well-worded but polite suggestions. And then there were others, none in the diplomatic core, who called a spade a spade.

I am too late to extend a formal thanks, but Dr. Vince Davis, Director, Patterson School of Diplomacy, University of Kentucky, was still around to read the first published edition; and I am sure that in some way unknown to us mortals, he will enjoy this latest edition. Vince read some of my early stories and, being an old AD pilot himself, encouraged me to continue to write. Vince died last year after a long battle with an illness that never prevented him from writing long letters of encouragement, not only to me, but to his many friends all over the world. He is greatly missed.

Vince Davis put me in touch with Colonel Garnett C.

Brown, Jr. "Charlie" Brown is one of the rare ones. He not only can fly the crates that airplanes come in, he also is an excellent editor and newspaper columnist. Charlie, no doubt, called Vince Davis to give him a piece of his mind when he discovered that some unknown Navy guy was sending him stories to read; however, being the gentleman that he is, he held his temper and read them. Charlie Brown's encouragement and sound writing suggestions provided one of the luckiest breaks I have had in my writing career. He convinced me that what I was writing was important and that some people would be interested in reading my stories. Charlie is a genius with words, even when you suspect that they are just words to make you feel good, but they were nice to hear and came when I needed them most. He can also move copy around and change a phrase here and there so that even the author begins to understand what he was trying to say. His teaching led to the rework of my manuscript so that an agent — who had told me two years before, after reading earlier versions, that her schedule was just too full to take me on as a client — offered me a contract the second time around. Thank you, Charlie Brown.

My agent is Janet Litherland. Her company, Write Choice Services, Inc., in Thomasville, Georgia, has grown by leaps and bounds because she has the talent and the patience to work with new writers like myself and pull readable stories from a jumble of words. Not only is she a great editor, she knows the publishing industry and how to get a new author published. Thanks, Janet! You have helped make an old man's later years a little more exciting than they would have otherwise been.

A special thanks to my old preflight buddy, Del Brandenburg. Del retired in the Washington, D.C., area, and his many trips to the National Archives and the Naval Historical Center saved me long hours of research. Many of the photographs in this book are there because of Del's patience and searching, not to mention his hours fighting Washington, D.C., traffic.

I also want to extend a heartfelt thanks to a more recently acquired buddy and great friend, Art Giberson. Art was an outstanding combat photographer in Vietnam and since that time has written and published many books, among them, *The Eyes of the Fleet, A History of Naval Photography*. Art spent many long hours copying, editing, and transmitting photographs for this book. Many are over fifty years old and required the touch of a master to restore a little of the sparkle originally in the persons and events they record. Thanks a million, Art!

Finally, I want to thank Mike Hardy for taking an interest in my book, and acquiring the rights after it was published elsewhere. His input and knowledge have brought great improvements. Thanks, Mike.

And thanks also to a whole bunch of other people who helped so very much by taking time to read early manuscripts and give encouragement. You know who you are — it would take another book to list all of you. Your comments as the years went by were more valuable than you can imagine. Especially those of you who called a spade a spade.

— Tex Atkinson
Gulf Breeze, Florida, 16 March 2004

About the Author

Kenneth W. "Tex" Atkinson spent most of his early years in and around his hometown of Hillsboro, Texas, where he attended high school and graduated shortly after the end of World War II. He then joined the Navy's flight program and after two years at Southwestern University in Georgetown, Texas, he entered Preflight in Pensacola, Florida.

Tex received his wings in 1949. He made five carrier cruises including two combat tours in Korea. He flew over a hundred combat missions and holds an assortment of military awards including the Distinguished Flying Cross.

His interest in literature began in school and peaked following the war when a roommate checked aboard the carrier with a collection of Hemingway, Faulkner, and Steinbeck novels. Later, Atkinson returned to college and graduated with a degree from the Medill School of Journalism at Northwestern University.

After naval service Tex settled his wife, Annie, and their six children in Pensacola, Florida, where he founded an employee benefits agency. His interest in aviation has remained strong all of his life, and for many years he and Annie traveled Florida on business for the agency in their small aircraft.

Tex has published numerous stories and articles related to aviation. *From The Cockpit* is his first book. Although retired, he remains active in civic affairs and enjoys speaking to audiences who are interested in hearing about Navy carrier pilots and the Korean War. Tex and Annie enjoy a large family and on occasion attempt to dispense wisdom, which is received mostly as humor by 22 grandchildren.